TABLE OF CONTENTS

ACRONYMS

ASB	Air-Sea Battle
ASEAN	Association of Southeast Asian Nations
CCP	Chinese Communist Party
COA	Course of Action
DoD	United States Department of Defense
EEZ	Exclusive Economic Zone
F-A-S-C-D	Feasible-Acceptable-Suitable-Complete-Distinguishable
FMS	United States Department of Defense Foreign Military Sales Program
INF	Intermediate-Range Nuclear Forces Treaty
MEU	U.S. Marine Expeditionary Unit
NATO	North Atlantic Treaty Organization
PLA	People's Liberation Army
PLAAF	People's Liberation Army Air Force
PLAN	People's Liberation Army Navy
PRC	People's Republic of China
ROK	Republic of Korea
SAC	PLA Second Artillery Corps
SAO	United States Department of Defense Security Assistance Operations
SCS	South China Sea
SSK	Conventionally-Powered Submarine
SSN	Nuclear-Powered Submarine
STANAGS	Standardization Agreements

TSOP	Theater-Shaping Operation
U.K.	United Kingdom
UN	United Nations
U.S.	United States
USAF	United States Air Force
USCENTCOM	United States Central Command
USD	U.S. Dollars
USMC	United States Marine Corps
USN	United States Navy
USPACOM	United States Pacific Command
USSOCOM	United States Special Operations Command
U.S.S.R.	Union of the Soviet Socialist Republics

CHAPTER 1

INTRODUCTION

We will play an essential role in promoting strong partnerships that strengthen the capabilities of the Pacific nations to defend and secure themselves.[1]
— U.S. Secretary of Defense Leon Panetta

After more than two decades of concentrated focus on the Middle East, United States (U.S.) military policy appears to be reconsidering its interests in the Pacific region.[2] This renewed Pacific regional interest gives particular emphasis on the contested waters of the South China Sea (SCS). The SCS region currently rates among the most economically important areas of the global maritime seascape and unsurprisingly, is the locus of competing claims of control. The U.S.'s role in the SCS region obviously must take into account U.S. goals and interests, but must also be considered in concert with the best assessments of the strategic thinking of the People's Republic of China (PRC), particularly given the PRC's emerging regional military ascendance with respect to its naval, air, and missile forces.[3]

---

[1]Leon E. Panetta, "Shangri-La Security Dialogue" (Speech presented at the Shangri-La Hotel, Singapore, 2 June 2012), http://www.defense.gov/Speeches/Speech.aspx?SpeechID=1681 (accessed 6 December 2012).

[2]Hillary Clinton, "America's Pacific Century," *Foreign Policy*, November 2011, http://www.foreignpolicy.com/articles/2011/10/11/americas_pacific_century?page=ful (accessed 6 December 2012).

[3]Anthony H. Cordesman and Robert M. Shelala II, "The FY2013 Defense Budget, the Threat of Defense Cuts and Sequestration and the Strategy-Reality Gap," Center for International and Strategic Studies, 12 June 2012, http://csis.org/publication/fy2013-defense-budget-and-new-strategy-reality-gap-0 (accessed 6 December 2012).

Problem Statement

Is the United States' present SCS regional engagement approach capable of addressing China's current and prospective policy and strategy; and if not, is there a better approach to maintaining the political *status quo* in the SCS region, one that shifts the defense burden to the regional powers?

To answer this question demands an examination in five dimensions: (1) a greater understanding of emerging trends in the region, (2) a clear assessment of the documentary evidence, (3) development of a workable strategic model, (4) applying the strategic model to determine the appropriate course of action, and (5) analyzing the collateral and contingent effects of the selected course of action.

Delimitations

For the purposes of this study, the equities and capabilities of Japan, India and Australia will not be considered. Additionally, Taiwan will only be explored in a limited fashion, due to its unique status.[4] The South China Sea, for the purposes of this study is defined as the body of water and its associated minor land features limited by 20 degrees North longitude running through the north part of Hainan Island, located between Vietnam, China, the Philippines, Singapore, and the north coasts of Indonesia. Also bordering the South China Sea are Malaysia and Brunei.

---

[4]Taiwan's situation is unique, complicating diplomatic and military engagement. Taiwan is diplomatically isolated, not even a state under the prevailing conventions of international law, is not an ASEAN member, and is unrecognized in status in multilateral negotiations. Taiwan nonetheless stakes specific regional claims and maintains physical possession of certain territories in the SCS region.

Chinese Military Modernization

In the aftermath of the Gulf War, Chinese defense analysts examined the United States' success against Saddam's Iraqi military--a military very similar to their own.[5] Since then, the Chinese People's Liberation Army (PLA) has modernized and diversified their ability to project military power in the SCS region. Recent U.S. defense studies have concluded that the PLA is becoming increasingly professional in every respect. As the PRC's military budget grows, the military leadership has been relinquishing some of their traditional political obligations to become more focused on their military duties.[6]

No longer a coastal defense force equipped with a hodgepodge of 1950s Soviet gear, the People's Liberation Army Navy (PLAN) now can field a variety of improved military equipment, including aircraft, naval vessels, and advanced missiles. Formerly the PLAN would improve imported weapons systems, but is now making great strides towards domesticating weapons production.[7] The PLAN is currently fielding a balanced naval force with new and enhanced operational capacities, including a carrier and improved amphibious ships. Their operational fleet consists of 79 destroyers and frigates, 50 submarines, 51 amphibious vessels, and 86 patrol craft. These units are divided into

---

[5]David Graff and Robin Higham, *A Military History of China*, 2nd ed. (Lexington: University Press of Kentucky, 2012), 287-288.

[6]Michael Kiselycznyk and Phillip C. Saunders, "Civil-Military Relations in China: Assessing the PLA's Role in Elite Politics," National Defense University, August 2010, http://www.ndu.edu/press/lib/pdf/china-perspectives/ChinaPerspectives-2.pdf (accessed 6 December 2012).

[7]Amy Chang and John Dotson, "Indigenous Weapons Development in China's Military Development" (Staff Research Report, *U.S.*-China Economic and Security Review Commission, 5 April 2012), http://www.uscc.gov/researchpapers/2012/China-Indigenous-Military-Dcvclopmcnts-Final-Draft-03-April2012.pdf (acccsscd 6 Dcccmbcr 2012).

three geographic fleet regions. The North Sea Fleet is generally focused on Japan and the Republic of Korea (ROK) in the north. The East Sea Fleet, focused upon Taiwan in the center, is homeported at Dinghai, Nanjing. The South Sea Fleet, homeported in Zianjiang, Guangzhou, is focused on the SCS. The combined combatants of the East and South Sea Fleets are 2 nuclear attack submarines (SSN), 30 conventionally powered attack subs (SSK), 16 destroyers (DDG), 40 frigates (FFGs), 67 missile armed patrol craft and 44 amphibious ships of various size.[8]

The PLAN recently gave sea trials to the refurbished Soviet carrier *Kuznetsov* purchased several years ago from Ukraine. However, that carrier is unique for its foreign origin--the majority of Chinese vessels in commission or currently under development are of Chinese design. Likewise, the modernization of the PLAN undersea force features Chinese designed and developed second- and third-generation nuclear submarines, including subs with nuclear-capable, intercontinental-ranged missiles.[9]

The PLAN modernization efforts are paralleled by the People's Liberation Army Air Force (PLAAF). Like their naval counterparts, in the 1990s the PLAAF transitioned from a hodgepodge of 1950s-vintage Soviet gear to a more modern force outfitted with new Russian and indigenous hardware. Since then, the PRC has continued to invest, transitioning the PLAAF from a limited strike and air defense roles into a far more balanced and capable force.[10]

---

[8]Office of the Secretary of Defense, "Annual Report to Congress: Military and Security Developments Involving the People's Republic of China 2012," May 2012, http://www.defense.gov/pubs/pdfs/2012_CMPR_Final.pdf (accessed 6 December 2012).

[9]Ibid.

[10]Ibid.

The PLAAF has also recently been pursuing considerably more out-of-area training. Since 2007, PLAAF training units have been deployed to Russia, Kazakhstan, Turkey, Pakistan, and Belarus.[11] Like the PLAN, much of this foreign engagement is focused on disaster relief and counter-terrorism operations, probably in an effort to ameliorate any suspicions of hostile motives. The PLAAF was also active in recent Chinese non-combatant evacuation operations and humanitarian assistance/disaster relief missions in Libya, Sudan, Pakistan, and Thailand.[12]

The PRC is dedicated to improving its airlift capacity, with more modern aircraft augmenting the PLAAF fleet of approximately three hundred transports. Moreover, the PRC's current quantitative advantages in combat aircraft are being enhanced by qualitative improvements in aircraft, weapons, and support. Current PRC modernization and procurement efforts include updating to a robust air defense capability, fielding advanced combat support aircraft, and the development of the PRC's first combat aircraft with low-observable characteristics--the stealthy Chengdu J-20. While much of the PLAAF's current known fleet of 1,570 fighters and 550 bomber/attack aircraft are no match for the latest Western designs, their less-capable aircraft are being replaced by highly capable ones.[13]

---

[11]Kenneth Allen and Emma Kelly, "Assessing the Growing PLA Air Force Foreign Relations Program," 26 April 2012, http://www.jamestown.org/single/?no_cache=1&tx_ttnews%5Btt_news%5D=39304 (accessed 6 December 2012).

[12]Ibid.

[13]Office of the Secretary of Defense, *Annual Report to Congress: Military and Security Developments Involving the People's Republic of China 2012*, May 2012, http://www.defense.gov/pubs/pdfs/2012_CMPR_Final.pdf (accessed 6 December 2012).

The PRC's missile program is a discrete military branch called the Second Artillery Corps (SAC). The SAC maintains the PRC's growing inventory of short-, medium-, intermediate-ranged, and intercontinental missiles. The SAC has likewise benefited from rapid advancements in Chinese technology, and fueled by the fast-growing Chinese economy. Today the SAC is one of the world's foremost missile forces.

Historically, the PRC maintained a small intercontinental ballistic missile deterrent force and fielded a variety of shorter-ranged missiles with conventional or nuclear capacity.[14] The development of anti-ship ballistic missiles in 2010 announced a mission-shift from U.S. nuclear deterrence to conventional deterrence through long-range attack capacity against the U.S. Navy (USN) fleet. Given the PRC's ongoing pursuit of improved defensive measures like base-hardening and increased road and rail mobility, the SAC is unquestionably a clear challenger to U.S. conventional-force superiority in the Pacific region.[15]

China's conventional forces are being buttressed by non-kinetic military capabilities of robust intelligence, surveillance, and reconnaissance assets, a capable cyber-espionage unit, and the burgeoning China National Space Administration's (CNSA) improved satellites and space delivery capability. In 2007, CNSA has also demonstrated kinetic military capabilities of an advanced anti-satellite weapons program (ASAT) through a test in that, while successful, was widely criticized for generating a

---

[14]Nuclear Threat Initiative, "Country Overview: China," November 2012, http://www.nti.org/country-profiles/china/ (accessed 6 December 2012).

[15]Mark Stokes, "China's Evolving Conventional Strategic Strike Capability," Project 2049 Institute, 14 September 2009, http://project2049.net/documents/ chinese_anti_ship_ballistic_missile_asbm.pdf (accessed 6 December 2012).

huge amount of hazardous orbiting debris.[16] In sum, China's across-the-board

modernization program should be seen as proof of their willingness to be a preeminent

player in both conventional and unconventional warfare.[17] This is a doctrine shift away

from Mao's "Peoples' War" to today's "high-tech local war."[18] Instead of a coastal force

dedicated limited objectives, the Chinese military is increasing capable of strategic and

expeditionary operations. The next logical area of defense interest to China is the South

China Sea, which is critical as Chinese owned territory, which sits astride critical sea

links to the outside world.

<u>Geo-Political Considerations</u>

The SCS is dominated by five major geographical features; the Paracel Islands,

the Spratly Islands, Pratas Islands, Scarborough Shoal, and the Macclesfield Bank.[19] A

number of smaller geographic features are also present; however, even these "major"

atolls and islands are very small, commonly having land, at high tide, of less than half a

square mile. In all, the regional landmass is roughly 200 islands. The PRC, Philippines,

Malaysia, Vietnam, and Brunei each have significant offshore claims or landmass stakes

---

[16]The test was the most destructive ever, creating an enormous quantity of hazardous space debris. See generally, T. S. Kelso, "Analysis of the 2007 Chinese ASAT Test and the Impact of its Debris on the Space Environment" (Technical Papers of the 2007 Advanced Maui Optical and Space Surveillance (AMOS) Technologies Conference, Maui 2007), http://www.centerforspace.com/downloads/files/pubs/AMOS-2007.pdf (accessed 6 December 2012).

[17]Office of the Secretary of Defense, *Annual Report to Congress: Military and Security Developments Involving the People's Republic of China 2012*, May 2012, http://www.defense.gov/pubs/pdfs/2012_CMPR_Final.pdf (accessed 6 December 2012).

[18]See Chapter 2 for an in-depth discussion of "high-tech local war."

[19]This paper will use the common English names for clarity.

in the SCS region. Further complicating the issue is "non-state" Taiwan's *de facto*

control[20] of certain regions. The United States remains involved in the area through a

series of diplomatic and historical links. Most notable is a mutual defense treaty with one

of the key players, the Republic of the Philippines.

<u>The Economic and Strategic Value of the SCS Region</u>

The economic value and strategic value of the SCS region in terms of its

importance to international shipping, its hydrocarbon reserves, and its fishing grounds is

significant. The SCS is the direct sea-shipping lane between largest economies of Asia

and their export markets in Europe, Africa, and India. The SCS region is also presumed

to have anywhere from rich to fantastically rich offshore oil and gas deposits. A U.S.

Geologic Survey estimates the region has 28 billion barrels of oil,[21] while a Chinese

estimate suggests more than 200 billion barrels, and the region's natural gas reserves are

estimated to be 900 trillion cubic feet.[22] These resources' convenient proximity to Asian

markets makes them obviously important to these energy-hungry states.

Currently, the SCS is one of the largest un-demarcated Exclusive Economic

Zones (EEZs) in the world. Control of the SCS fishing grounds and their accompanying

---

[20]This paper will reference Taiwan's *de facto* control where necessary for clarity; however, Taiwan's *de jure* status is undefined by the U.S. Government. See Shirley A. Kan, "China/Taiwan: Evolution of the "One China" Policy-Key Statements from Washington, Beijing, and Taipei," Congressional Research Service, 24 June 2011, http://www.fas.org/sgp/crs/row/RL30341.pdf (accessed 6 December 2012).

[21]U.S. Energy Information Administration, Country Analysis Briefs, "South China Sea," March 2008, http://www.eia.gov/EMEU/cabs/South_China_Sea/pdf.pdf (accessed 6 December 2012).

[22]Ibid.

EEZs are presently, and will remain a lucrative economic prize, provided they can be sustainably managed.

<u>The Nature of the Competing Claims; Economic and Territorial</u>

In their current incarnation, the competing claims to the SCS are almost 75 years old. Regional claims generally come in two types; (1) claims to landmass territory like the islands, shoals, and reefs, and (2) off-landmass EEZ claims. An EEZ grants the claimant sole economic use of the ocean and seafloor to 200 nautical miles (370 kilometers) from its territorial shore. Typically, overlapping EEZ claims are settled bilaterally between the competing claimants. The confused array of EEZ claims in the South China Sea has rendered typical settlement impossible. Territorial claims necessarily overlap with EEZ claims. Once territorial ownership is settled, an EEZ claim may be staked. Thus, any new territorial claims can potentially affect several other claims and can have similar far-reaching repercussions. Moreover, the maritime demarcation and enforcement of claims can be problematic and rarely coincident with natural features like oil fields or fishing grounds.

The PRC, Vietnam, and the Philippines constitute the bulk of the settled multi-lateral landmass claims to the SCS region, while the Malaysian and Brunei's established claims are more limited. Indonesia has no territorial claims but has a diplomatic stake in regional stability. Singapore is most concerned with sea-going transit rights, being economically dependent upon ocean-going trade. Taiwan maintains military forces on certain northern islands.

The three major landmass territories in dispute are the Spratly Islands, Paracel Islands, and Scarborough Shoal. The Spratly Islands are claimed in their entirety by the

PRC, Taiwan, and Vietnam; claimed in part by the Philippines, Malaysia, and Brunei; and occupied in part by all involved except Brunei. The Paracel Islands are claimed by both the PRC and Vietnam, and occupied by the PRC. The Scarborough Shoal is claimed by the PRC, the Philippines, and Taiwan.[23] Each of these regional players, as individual nations and diplomatic associations, shall be examined later.

China's Claims in the SCS Region

There is a compelling argument[24] that the Chinese feel hindered by "geographic containment" of the various island chains; which is to say, the islands constrict the flow of trade in and out of China, and significantly limit its power projection.[25] China's economy depends on its ability to maintain an outlet to the oceanic trade, and the PRC has feared encirclement for much of the last century. The conclusion of the Second World War encouraged the Chinese government to pursue some longstanding but dormant territorial claims within China's historical sphere of influence. These expansive claims included nearly all of sovereign Mongolia and about ninety percent of the SCS region. These vast claims in the SCS region were originally promulgated by the Republic

---

[23]Ronald O'Rourke, "Maritime Territorial and Exclusive Economic Zone (EEZ) Disputes Involving China: Issues for Congress," *Congressional Research Service,* 22 October 2012, http://www.fas.org/sgp/crs/row/R42784.pdf (accessed 6 December 2012).

[24]Struye de Swielande, "The Reassertion of the United States in the Asia-Pacific Region," *Parameters* (Spring 2012), http://www.carlisle.army.mil/USAWC/parameters/ Articles/2012spring/Struye_de_Swielande.pdf (accessed 6 December 2012).

[25]Ibid., 78.

of China in 1948 and are known colloquially as the "Nine Dotted Line," (also the "U-shape Line").[26]

During the first half of the twentieth century, China's military weakness undermined their ability to enforce their claims to the Paracel and Spratly islands, although they began to actively garrison forces on these claims in the early 1960s. The conflict among various claimants to these territories reached its peak in the 1974 naval engagement of then South Vietnam and the PRC. This was only a prelude to continual naval skirmishing that occurred in the area for nearly another decade.[27]

In the 1990s, the issue simmered while the SCS region gained increasing prominence. By the 2000s, Beijing became increasingly assertive. Invoking their Nine Dotted Line claim, the PRC engaged in a series of naval provocations with the Philippines, Vietnam, and India. China currently maintains this provocative and assertive posture by intercepting non-Chinese vessels operating in contested areas.[28]

---

[26]This paper will apply the former term. See Hong Nong, "Interpreting the U-shape Line in the South China Sea," *China-US Focus*, 15 May 2012, http://www.chinausfocus.com/peace-security/interpreting-the-u-shape-line-in-the-south-china-sea/ (accessed 6 December 2012).

[27]There is a history of Sino-Vietnamese conflict; in January 1974, a South Vietnamese Navy flotilla clashed with a Chinese Navy force, resulting the Chinese physical possession of the Paracel Islands. In 1979, the Sino-Vietnamese border war caused more than 20 thousand casualties. In 1988, Chinese and Vietnamese forces engaged at the Johnson South Reef, causing nearly all parties on the islands to engage in further fortification.

[28] Indian Express, "Chinese warship confronts Indian Navy vessel in disputed zone: report," 1 September 2011, http://www.financialexpress.com/news/chinese-warship-confronts-indian-navy-vessel-in-disputed-zone-report/840151 (accessed 6 December 2012).

The Claims of ASEAN Nations

The Association of Southeast Asian Nations (ASEAN)[29] was developed as a voluntary membership organization "[t]o promote regional peace and stability . . . and mutual assistance on matters of common interest in the economic, social, cultural, technical, scientific and administrative fields."[30] Subsequently, ASEAN adopted this statement of "Fundamental Principles:"[31]

> Mutual respect for the independence, sovereignty, equality, territorial integrity, and national identity of all nations; The right of every State to lead its national existence free from external interference, subversion or coercion; Non-interference in the internal affairs of one another; Settlement of differences or disputes by peaceful manner; Renunciation of the threat or use of force; and Effective cooperation among themselves.

ASEAN's Fundamental Principles statement addresses the competing claims in the SCS region, and shares the U.S. policy of preferring the status quo to aggressive or coercive redrawing of regional borders. While ASEAN has emerged as the *de facto* regional diplomatic collective, its mutual defense agreements are non-existent.[32]

---

[29]ASEAN is composed of Indonesia, Malaysia, the Philippines, Singapore, Thailand, Brunei, Burma (Myanmar), Cambodia, Laos, and Vietnam.

[30]Colloquially, "the ASEAN Way"--their charter stresses the non-interference in member states internal affairs. See official charter, http://www.asean.org/archive/publications/ASEAN-Charter.pdf (accessed 6 December 2012).

[31]Ibid.

[32]Derek Pham, "On to the Hard Stuff: An ASEAN Defense Community?" Center for Strategic and International Studies, 9 May 2011, http://cogitasia.com/on-to-the-hard-stuff-an-asean-defense-community/ (accessed 6 December 2012).

The PRC (which is not a member of ASEAN) has several rivals to its claims in the region and, except Taiwan, each of those rivals is a member of ASEAN.[33] Four of the ten members of ASEAN have claims in the SCS; it is likely ASEAN will emerge as the unified voice of diplomatic engagement with the PRC.

ASEAN, however, remains crippled by infighting on the SCS issue. A recent example was the effort to adopt of a binding "Code of Conduct" with respect to the SCS region. A previous 2002 declaration signed by both ASEAN and the PRC was voluntary and did little preclude subsequent regional hostilities. ASEAN's purpose was to craft a workable diplomatic solution that buttressed its members' unitary strength even as it blunted the PRC's ability to drive individual member states into bilateral negotiations that tend to put the weaker party at a disadvantage.

The ASEAN members most invested in a highly specific declaration (that is, the Philippines and Vietnam) disagreed with the nation most interested in a flexible declaration, likely due to its close relationship with the PRC (that is, Cambodia), which caused an acrimonious end to the 2012 discussions[34] despite significant Filipino concessions.[35] Aggressive diplomacy by Indonesia managed to salvage parts of the agreement, but ASEAN members remain vulnerable to being forced into disadvantageous bilateral negotiations with the PRC. It is likely that all the ASEAN member states would

---

[33]A ten-nation regional diplomatic and economic membership organization dedicated to pursuing mutual goals of economic growth, social progress, cultural development, and protection of regional peace and stability.

[34]Carlyle A. Thayer, "ASEAN'S Code of Conduct in the South China Sea: A Litmus Test for Community-Building?" http://www.japanfocus.org/-Carlyle_A_-Thayer/3813 (accessed 6 December 2012).

[35]Ibid.

prefer ASEAN's role to enlarge, so the member states may collectively speak with a more powerful voice.

Since 1946, Vietnam has vigorously maintained its claims in the SCS region. Thirty years of Chinese politico-military support to Hanoi muted, but did not resolve, any conflicting claims; instead, this special relationship may have prolonged the conflict. Indeed, the uneasy Sino-Vietnamese Communist partnership forged in the 1950s, and its unfortunate outcome, ultimately gave rise to profound and mutual feelings of betrayal and animosity, which no doubt underlies much of the hostility regarding their competing claims in the SCS region.[36]

Despite this animosity, Hanoi and Beijing retain substantial political, military, and economic connections. Considering that the purpose of Deng's war with Vietnam in 1979 may have been to set boundaries for acceptable Vietnamese behavior, rather than achieving any particular military objective.[37] Beijing now seems willing, within the bilateral Sino-Vietnamese relationship, to generally accept Vietnamese autonomy in its dealings with the U.S.[38] Vietnam has embarked on a recent naval buildup with significant

---

[36]This animosity is also amplified by the 1979 Sino-Vietnamese War, and by conflict between the Vietnamese and Chinese navies over the South China Sea. See Lorenz M. Lüthi, "Beyond Betrayal: Beijing, Moscow, and the Paris Negotiations, 1971–1973," *Journal of Cold War Studies* 11, no. 1 (Winter 2009): 57-107.

[37]Xiaoming Zhang, "China's 1979 War with Vietnam: A Reassessment," *The China Quarterly* 184 (December 2005): 851-874.

[38]This represents a significant and welcome policy departure for Beijing, insofar as history provides evidence that the PRC did not object to Vietnamese independence, yet took great exception to Hanoi's growing relationship with the U.S.S.R. when it was a competing superpower. See Nicholas Khoo, "Breaking the Ring of Encirclement: The Sino-Soviet Rift and Chinese Policy toward Vietnam, 1964–1968," *Journal of Cold War Studies* 12 (2010): 3-42.

weapons purchases from Russia purchasing six Kilo-class submarines, along with Gepard class missile frigates. Recent conflict, historical animosity, and a shared border render the Sino-Vietnamese relationship a potential flashpoint.

Manila (with perhaps a forgivable excess of optimism) calls the South China Sea, "The West Philippine Sea." The Republic of the Philippines maintains substantial territorial and EEZ claims within the region.[39] These claims, from World War II onward, were bolstered by substantial U.S. air and naval presence at large bases such as Subic Bay, Clark Air Force Base, and a number of smaller airfields and naval facilities mostly around Manila. In the wake of the Cold War, Filipino nationalistic demands eventually led to the shuttering of those bases by the early 1990s. By 1999, however, the Philippines were once again hosting large bilateral exercises with the U.S.[40] Since then, new Filipino realities, like the emerging threat from domestic Islamist terrorism, have provided fresh incentives to forge a new U.S.-Philippines military partnership, including a renewed interest in hosting a U.S. military presence.

The Philippines' naval and air forces lack any modern combatant surface vessels or aircraft.[41] While the Philippine government is certainly ramping up military spending,

---

[39]D. J. Yap, "Aquino to US: Speak up on West PH Sea," *Philippine Daily Inquirer*, 20 November 2012, http://globalnation.inquirer.net/57120/aquino-to-us-speak-up-on-west-ph-sea (accessed 6 December 2012).

[40]Jason Gutierrez, "Philippines sees Subic port as vital to US interests," *Agence-Press France,* 8 October 2012, http://www.abs-cbnnews.com/global-filipino/world/10/08/12/philippines-sees-subic-port-vital-us-interests (accessed 6 December 2012).

[41]As of August 2012, the Philippine Air Force has yet to replace its last jet aircraft it decommissioned in 2005. The Philippine Navy has two former US Coast Guard cutters and another on order. The cutters current lack any significant anti-air or anti-submarine capability.

the military is being required to shift from a total focus on counter-insurgency towards conventional combat. The U.S. has provided a robust anti-terrorism training assistance mission and assisted Filipino forces fighting Islamist insurgencies in the south. Beijing's competing territorial and economic claims, while a less immediate threat to the Philippines than insurgencies, have driven Manila to reconsider the value of hosting a U.S. military presence.

Kuala Lumpur's diplomatic relationship with Beijing is arguably the most civil of all the regional powers. This civility is almost certainly informed by the fact that, unlike Vietnam and the Philippines, Malaysia and China have never engaged in direct armed conflict.[42] Likewise, Kuala Lumpur routinely makes it a point to emphasize parity in its relations with both Washington and Beijing. For instance, while the PRC is Malaysia's largest trading partner, its defense relationship with the U.S. has proven exceptionally durable.

Malaysia is a party to the Five Power Defense Arrangements, with the U.K., Australia, New Zealand, and the city-state of Singapore.[43] The Arrangement requires multilateral consultation in the event of an attack on peninsular Malaysia. However, in peacetime the Arrangement accommodates integrated air defense systems, training exercises, and other training opportunities. Recently, Kuala Lumpur has made the compelling argument that ASEAN members should first settle their competing regional territorial and EEZ claims by themselves, to improve ASEAN's negotiating position with

---

[42]China did support a Communist insurgency in the area in the 1950s and 1960s.

[43]Damon Bristow, "The Five Power Defence Arrangements: Southeast Asia's Unknown Regional Security Organization," *Contemporary Southeast Asia: A Journal of International and Strategic Affairs* 27, no. 1 (2005): 1-20.

Beijing.[44] The Royal Malaysian Navy's largest surface combatants are missile-armed frigates and maintains two French-built Scorpène-class submarines. The Royal Malaysian Air Force maintains a small but credible strike and maritime patrol capability. Kuala Lumpur is the regional power most likely to pursue the *status quo* to avoid having to take either Beijing's or Washington's side.

Brunei's claims in the SCS region are limited to a few small EEZ claims in the southern party of the Spratly Islands. Brunei makes no claim to the Paracels. Brunei maintains limited military forces, so it lacks the resources to physically possess the territory supporting those EEZ claims. The Royal Brunei Navy has limited deep-water capability, and is mainly focused on protection of offshore oil facilities. The Royal Brunei Air Force has no fixed-wing strike capability. Brunei will probably continue to maintain its SCS claims diplomatically to preserve its right to participate in any prospective settlement. Like Malaysia, Brunei is one of the ASEAN members advocating unity to strengthen ASEAN's collective negotiating power.

Jakarta maintains no claims to territory within the SCS region, but as the largest ASEAN member in population and territorial area, Indonesia has a great stake in regional security. Like Kuala Lumpur, Jakarta currently pursues a policy of parity in its relations with both Washington and Beijing. The policy has proven prudent, as both Sino-Indonesian and U.S.-Indonesian relations have improved considerably, particularly since

---

[44]"Asean Urged To Unite Over South China Sea," 14 August 2012, http://bruneiembassy.be/asean-urged-to-unite-over-south-china-sea/ (accessed 6 December 2012).

the 1990s.[45] Even so, Jakarta retains a level of distrust towards the United States, arising from this strained diplomatic history. Similarly, Jakarta has justifiable concerns about China's "soft power" to influence and mobilize Indonesia's marginalized but relatively affluent ethnic Chinese population.[46] Politically, Indonesia is likely to continue pursuing a diplomatic policy of "dynamic equilibrium," downplaying any superpower rivalry in the area, boosting its own regional standing, and maintaining its maximum freedom of agency.[47] Jakarta has enhanced its security position by prodigiously increasing defense spending, including purchasing three submarines from South Korea.[48] These submarines will join Indonesia's fleet of six missile armed frigates, two other submarines, and a number of smaller surface ships. However, Indonesia's military buildup is functionally undermined by Jakarta's decision to pursue a defense procurement program that can charitably be described as "eclectically sourced."[49]

---

[45]Indonesia was diplomatically isolated from both the U.S. and China during the Cold War.

[46]Greta Nabbs-Keller, "The Strategic Implications of Closer China-Indonesia Relations," *Security Challenges* 7, no. 1 (2011): 23-41, www.securitychallenges. org.au/ArticlePDFs/vol7no3Nabbs-Keller.pdf (accessed 6 December 2012).

[47]Prashanth Parameswaran, "The Limits to Sino-Indonesian Relations," *China Brief* 12, no. 8, (2012): 2, http://www.jamestown.org/uploads/media/cb_04_02.pdf (accessed 6 December 2012).

[48]From USD $2.6 billion in 2006, to USD $8 billion in 2012. See The Economist, "Shopping Spree," 24 March 2012, http://www.economist.com/node/21551056 (accessed 6 December 2012).

[49]Trefor Moss, "Indonesian Military Powers Up," *The Diplomat,* 18 January 2012, http://thediplomat.com/flashpoints-blog/2012/01/18/indonesia-military-powers-up/ (accessed 6 December 2012).

<u>The U.S.'s Role in the SCS region and its Force Posture in the Pacific</u>

The U.S. Government takes no official position on the various claims in the SCS region, but insists the resolution of competing claims must be accomplished without force or coercion.[50] While Washington continues to call for diplomatic solutions, it has also announced a redeployment of combat power to the Pacific, with plans for nearly sixty percent of the USN to be based in Pacific within next decade.[51] Official pronouncements discreetly refused to name the PRC as the object of this force rebalancing, but it is well-understood that the rise of Chinese military power was the prime motivator.

By any measure, the U.S. already maintains a large force posture in the Pacific, principally arising from its longstanding treaty obligations with both the ROK and Japan. About 20 percent of U.S. military forces are already based in the Pacific, roughly 325,000 personnel. The USN maintains 6 of 10 carrier battle groups--about 180 ships--and roughly 100,000 personnel. The USMC maintains about 65 percent of its total combat strength in the Pacific; roughly 85,000 personnel divided between 2 Marine Expeditionary Forces. The U.S. Army fields 5 Stryker Brigades in the Pacific, comprising about 60,000 personnel. The USAF maintains 400 aircraft and 40,000 personnel. The

---

[50]Ronald O'Rourke, "Maritime Territorial and Exclusive Economic Zone (EEZ) Disputes Involving China: Issues for Congress," Congressional Research Service, 22 October 2012, http://www.fas.org/sgp/crs/row/R42784.pdf (accessed 6 December 2012).

[51]This represents a substantial departure from the policy in place since the Second World War where forces have been evenly divided between Pacific and Atlantic. See British Broadcasting Corporation, "Leon Panetta: US to Deploy 60% of Navy Fleet to Pacific," 1 June 2012, http://www.bbc.co.uk/news/world-us-canada-18305750 (accessed 6 December 2012).

USSOCOM contingent is roughly 1,200 Special Operations Forces.[52] U.S. bases in the Pacific are concentrated in Hawaii, Japan-Okinawa, Guam, and the ROK.

Washington is contemplating diversifying its basing structure, even to the extent of considering refurbishing derelict airfields from World War II, such as Baker Airfield on Tinian Island.[53] Naturally, economic considerations are relevant--particularly the willingness and ability of host nations to share base's expenses.[54] While several of the regional powers have encouraged U.S. military presence in the SCS as a check-and-balance against China there are almost certainly limitations to what U.S. can functionally accomplish on behalf of these nations and in its own interests.[55]

Historically, the U.S. has eschewed a focused strategy, choosing to establish a broad spectrum of programs that address at nearly every conceivable threat.[56] While this approach has certainly been effective in building a peerless capacity to wage global war,

---

[52]U.S. Pacific Command, "USPACOM Facts," http://www.pacom.mil/about-uspacom/facts.shtml (accessed 6 December 2012).

[53]Joshua Keating, "U.S. reopening World War II bases in Pacific," *Foreign Policy*, 5 June 2012, http://blog.foreignpolicy.com/posts/2012/06/05/us_reopening_world_war_ii_bases_in_pacific (accessed 6 December 2012).

[54]Hana Katusmoto, "U.S., Japan sign new five-year 'host nation support' agreement," *Stars and Stripes,* 21 January 2011, http://www.stripes.com/news/pacific/japan/u-s-japan-sign-new-five-year-host-nation-support-agreement-1.1324281 citing Japan's agreement to USD $2 billion in defense cost-sharing (accessed 6 December 2012).

[55]Frank Langfitt, "America's Asian Allies Question Its Staying Power," *National Public Radio,* 22 October 2012, http://m.npr.org/story/163378356 (accessed 6 December 2012).

[56]Paul Darling and Justin Lawlor, "Married to Clausewitz, but Sleeping with Jomini, How Operational Concepts Masquerade as Strategy, and Why They Must," *Infinity Journal* 2, no. 3 (Summer 2012): 21-24.

it is no longer economically sustainable. Budgets will increasingly be a significant constraint. It is unlikely the U.S. military defense budget will even accommodate maintenance of the *status quo*. Indeed, it is likely U.S. defense spending will stagnate, and even more likely, be substantially slashed.[57]

There is a stark mismatch between Beijing's and Washington's regional visions of the sanctity of global commons and the maintenance of the current order. Caught in between are the South China Sea regional powers, who will be expected to compromise or choose sides, knowing their interests will play a relatively minor role in Beijing and Washington's contest of wills. An examining the relevant literature will focus the likely Chinese and U.S. objectives in the SCS. By comparing this understanding of the U.S. and China in the SCS with a historical case-study of U.S. and British in the Persian Gulf region, we can determine relevant similarities of models of outside military engagement. The application of these models can provide a useful methodology and potential template for the development of mechanism for future regional engagement in the SCS. Regional engagement concepts require in turn an examination of their feasibility, acceptability, suitability among other factors to achieve U.S. national security goals.

---

[57]Cordesman and Shelala.

CHAPTER 2

LITERATURE REVIEW

To gain insight in the ongoing and prospective goals and strategy of the United States and the People's Republic of China, it is necessary to study both nation's historical and current motives and strategies. A comparison of both Chinese and U.S. strategy can also illustrate areas of potential conflict.

In attempting to create a model of regional engagement for the U.S., research on a similar model is worthy of study. Successful application of that model will show how the model succeeded and failed under those circumstances, and whether the model remains, on the whole, extensible and applicable to the current problem.

Chinese Government Publications

Substantial and authoritative documentary evidence exists to inform a well-reasoned assessment of Chinese military strategy. Beijing publishes an annual *China's National Defense* report,[58] colloquially known as the "China Defense White Paper," analogous to Washington's *U.S. Defense Strategic Guidance*. *The Science of Military Strategy* is the most comprehensive and authoritative single volume on the topic, and arguably the work most representative of excellence of current Chinese military

---

[58]Describing the Asia Pacific as "generally stable" but "intricate" and "volatile." See Information Office of the State Council of the People's Republic of China, "China's National Defense in 2010," 31 March 2011, http://www.china.org.cn/government/whitepaper/node_7114675.htm (accessed 6 December 2012).

thinking.[59] The White Paper[60] lays out the official goals and strategic view of the PRC government. While neither lengthy nor descriptive, the White Paper does provide Beijing's four-point defense strategy; [61] (1) Safeguarding national sovereignty, security, and interests of national development, (2) Maintaining social harmony and stability, (3) Accelerating the modernization of national defense and the armed forces, (4) Maintaining world peace and stability.

The White Paper also updates PLA's current military modernization program and provides a progress report regarding Beijing's bilateral and multi-lateral diplomacy. ASEAN is addressed directly, but Beijing's SCS claims are not.[62] *The Science of Military Strategy* is edited by Major General Peng Guangqian and Major General Yao Youzhi, who also serve as advisers to the PRC's powerful Central Military Commission and the PRC's Politburo Standing Committee. *The Science of Military Strategy* describes the strategic situation from the PRC's perspective and offers guidance in a very prescriptive fashion. The volume persuasively argues that nuclear weapons proliferation renders modern war technologically dynamic, violent, yet limited in scope. The volume then

---

[59]LTC Tim Thomas (ret.), "The Chinese Military's Strategic Mindset," *Military Review* (November-December 2007): 47. http://www.au.af.mil/au/awc/awcgate/ milreview/thomas_china_mind-set.pdf (accessed 6 December 2012).

[60]Information Office of the State Council of the People's Republic of China, "China's National Defense in 2010," 31 March 2011, http://www.china.org.cn/ government/whitepaper/node_7114675.htm (accessed 6 December 2012).

[61]Ibid.

[62]Ibid.

operationalizes this concept, describing it as "high-tech local war."[63] Effectively, high-tech local war analyzes the operating environment then synthesizes conventional military operations, technology, politics, and diplomacy.

One example of how the high-tech local war concept is being implemented is the Yulin Naval Base on strategically significant Hainan Island. The previously secret base was brought to the public attention by the Federation of American Scientists in 2008. It features substantial underground facilities and special high-tech operational capacities including degaussing facilities to lower the magnetic signature of submarines and ships.[64] Another example of high-tech local war implementation is the SAC's vast underground tunnel complex, (dubbed, "The Underground Great Wall") capable of housing a larger inventory of tactical and strategic missiles than heretofore suspected.[65] While there has been criticism of the Karber study's methodologies, an extensive Chinese tunneling effort has been public knowledge since the 1990s.[66] While *The Science of Military Strategy* does not mention the SCS by name, it does say the defense of Chinese territory is a core military mission, and Beijing claims offshore islands within its territory.

---

[63]People's Liberation Army (Academy of Military Sciences, trans.), *The Science of Military Strategy,* ed. Peng Guangquian and Yao Youzhi (Beijing: Military Science Publishing House, 2005), iv.

[64]Hans M. Kristensen, "New Chinese SSBN Deploys to Hainan Island," *Federation of American Scientists,* 24 April 2008, http://www.fas.org/blog/ssp/2008/04/new-chinese-ssbn-deploys-to-hainan-island-naval-base.php (accessed 6 December 2012).

[65]Phillip A. Karber, "Strategic Implications of China's Underground Great Wall," 26 September 2011, http://www.fas.org/nuke/guide/china/Karber_UndergroundFacilities-Full_2011_reduced.pdf (accessed 6 December 2012).

[66]Tong Zhou, "Deterrence Meets a Great Wall," *The Diplomat*, 9 November 2011, http://thediplomat.com/new-leaders-forum/2011/11/09/deterrence-meets-great-wall/ (accessed 6 December 2012).

Fears of containment play a part in Chinese pronouncements, with "hegemonism" as the prime threat to global stability. With the fall of the Soviet Union, China analysts clearly see the U.S. as a great and potentially unconstrained global power.[67] Primary sources suggest that China's strategy in the SCS will likely involve putting slow pressure on weaker regional powers to convince them to abandon their competing claims on what Beijing views as rightfully Chinese territory, while signaling that the costs of U.S. intervention will outweigh any benefit. The modernization of Chinese military forces, especially air and naval ones provides the PRC with much more effective means of defense against U.S. power. It also provides the means for the Chinese to defend their regional claims.

U.S. Strategy

U.S. PACOM Strategy towards China is in the following documents.

National Security Strategy

The White House's publication *National Security Strategy* explains the rationale underlying the Obama Administration's "pivot" to the Pacific. This national security strategy model stands on four interests; security, prosperity, values, and the strengthening of international order.[68] This strategy document also specifically addresses Washington's intent to enhance its contacts with ASEAN, the Pacific regional powers, and Beijing.

---

[67]Wang Jisi, "Multipolarity Versus Hegemonism: Chinese Views of International Politics," China Institute of Science and Management, 28 September 2008, www.cssm.gov.cn/view.php?id=21083 (accessed 6 December 2012).

[68]Office of the President of the United States, *National Security Strategy*, May 2010, http://www.whitehouse.gov/sites/default/files/rss_viewcr/national_security_strategy.pdf (accessed 6 December 2012).

Included with a desire with actively engage with Asian powers like ASEAN and China, the U.S. commits itself to the protection and advancement of a just international order that allows access to the "global commons, and strengthens partners."[69]

Defense Strategic Guidance

The Department of Defense's official strategy guide, *Sustaining U.S. Global Leadership: Priorities for 21st Century Defense,*[70] defines the U.S. military's missions. "[W]hile the U.S. military will continue to contribute to security globally, *we will of necessity rebalance toward the Asia-Pacific region.* U.S. relationships with Asian allies and key partners are critical to the future stability and growth of the region."[71] These missions require the capacity to both "deter and defeat aggression" and "strengthen international and regional security."[72] Less clear are how these links are intended to be forged and how such links synergistically build partner capacity or provide deterrent effect. Of the ten missions presented, half ("Deter and Defeat Aggression," "Project Power Despite Anti-Access/Area Denial Challenges," "Operate Effectively in Space and Cyberspace," "Maintain a Safe, Secure, and Effective Nuclear Deterrent," "Conduct

---

[69]Ibid., 14, 43.

[70]U.S. Department of Defense, *Sustaining U.S. Global Leadership: Priorities for 21st Century Defense*, January 2012, 10, www.defense.gov/news/Defense_Strategic_ Guidance.pdf (accessed 6 December 2012).

[71]Ibid., 2 (emphasis in original).

[72]In total, the four objectives are "Counter Violent Extremism, Deter and Defeat Aggression, Strengthen International and Regional Security, Shape the Future Force." See U.S. Department of Defense, *National Military Strategy*, 2011, http://www.jcs.mil// content/files/2011-02/020811084800_2011_NMS_-_08_FEB_2011.pdf (accessed 6 December 2012).

Humanitarian, Disaster Relief, and Other Operations" are directed at China and/or sea control.[73]

Cooperative Strategy for 21st Century Seapower

The United States Navy has recently expanded its vision of global presence and regional engagement in the maritime strategy document *Cooperative Strategy for 21st Century Seapower,*[74] colloquially "CS-21." This strategy maintains the sea commons are vital to global economic welfare, and the U.S. Navy, Marines, and Coast Guard, must be regionally focused, that is, "forward deployed and engaged in mutually beneficial relationships with regional and global partners." to preempt conflict. Throughout this document, the U.S. Navy commits itself to the continuing maintenance of access and security on the world's oceans.

USPACOM Strategic Guidance

The U.S. Pacific Command's (USPACOM) mission "promotes regional security and deters aggression; and, if deterrence fails, is prepared to respond to the full spectrum

---

[73]U.S. Department of Defense, *Sustaining U.S. Global Leadership: Priorities for 21st Century Defense*, January 2012, 10-12, www.defense.gov/news/Defense_ Strategic_Guidance.pdf (accessed 6 December 2012).

[74]Department of the Navy, *Cooperative Strategy for 21st Century Seapower*, October 2007, 12, http://www.navy.mil/maritime/Maritimestrategy.pdf (accessed 6 December 2012).

of military contingencies to restore Asia-Pacific stability and security."[75] This strategy focuses on building partner capability and conflict-deterrence.[76]

Commissioned by the Office of the Secretary of Defense, The Center for Strategic and International Studies report, *U.S. Force Posture Strategy in the Asia Pacific Region: An Independent Assessment* implies that U.S. force posture in the Pacific is as much a function of years of inertia as the product of a coordinated plan.[77] This report calls the U.S. forward deployed posture critical but expensive and notes it is likely to face increasing resource competition.[78]

This report recommends roughly the same force structure, and also focuses upon the U.S. defense commitments to Japan and the ROK, presenting three options: increased, decreased, and steady-state regional force investment. The report also argues that the Pacific needs forces focused on the ability to respond along the range of military operations, particularly theater-shaping operations (TSOPs).[79] However, in this report's view, TSOP is effectively restricted to participation in military exercises.[80] Future

---

[75]U.S. Pacific Command, "About Us," http://www.pacom.mil/

[76]ADM Robert Willard, USN, "United States Pacific Command Strategic Guidance," http://www.pacom.mil/about-uspacom/strategic-guidance.shtml (accessed 6 December 2012).

[77]David J. Berteau and Michael J. Green, "U.S. Force Posture Strategy in the Asia Pacific Region: An Independent Assessment," Center for Strategic and International Studies, August 2012, 5, htp://csis.org/files/publication/120814_FINAL_PACOM_optimized.pdf (accessed 6 December 2012).

[78]Ibid.

[79]See Chapter 4 for an in-depth explanation of theater-shaping operations.

[80]Ibid.

assessments of force structure are not focused upon either the SCS or non-traditional means of engagement with partners in the area.

Theater-Shaping Operations

Official U.S. pronouncements on its security posture in Asia[81] routinely emphasize the value of theater-shaping operations (TSOPs) as they also stress the value of forging effective cooperative security relationships. Admiral Samuel J. Locklear described the wide-ranging benefits of TSOPs[82] as enhancing regional security; thereby permitting enhanced trade, which economically benefits all regional powers--even powers that are U.S. rivals. TSOPs in the SCS region must meet three goals. (1) TSOPs need to clearly demonstrate U.S. defense commitment to the partnered nation/s. (2) these TSOPs efforts must create new deterrents or amplify existing ones. (3) the U.S. must design TSOPs with the expectation that partner nations will bear their own defense burdens.

AirSea Battle

In 2010, the Pentagon publicly announced "AirSea Battle" as the new U.S. operational framework for major combat operations. While AirSea Battle is, in theory, an operational concept applicable to various theaters, it is commonly understood by the

---

[81]Office of the President of the United States, *National Security Strategy*, May 2010, 42, http://www.whitehouse.gov/sites/default/files/rss_viewer/ national_security_strategy.pdf (accessed 6 December 2012).

[82]Donna Miles, "Locklear: Pacom's Priorities Reflect New Strategic Guidance," *American Forces Press Service*, 12 May 2012, www.defense.gov/news/ newsarticle.aspx?id=116397 (accessed 6 December 2012).

defense community to be a specific response to the growing capabilities of the PRC, tailored to the needs of the Pacific region.

AirSea Battle is a joint operation between the USN and United States Air Force (USAF) intended to address China's increasingly complex anti-access/area-denial capability. AirSea Battle is built around a variety of networked sensors and weapons platforms capable of neutralizing Chinese forces--systems that will be required should the United States face a militarily modern opponent.[83] The AirSea Battle, in its unclassified presentations, uses China as the most stressing case for the U.S. to operate against in wartime. Implicit in this is the lessening of U.S. deterrence capability as Chinese military capability improves.

In its unclassified form, AirSea Battle is a two-phase campaign. In Phase 1 the U.S. would ride out the initial attack then attempt to blind their intelligence, surveillance, and reconnaissance capabilities, then the U.S. would engage in missile suppression campaign to limit enemy deep-strike capability--specifically ballistic and cruise missiles[84]--which would theoretically permit the U.S. to seize the initiative and move on to the next phase. In Phase 2, the U.S. would commence a deep blockade operation to limit enemy offensive operations; U.S. activities would focus on logistically sustaining air, sea, and space operations while ramping up capability for sustaining this operation

[83]Jan van Tol, et. al., "AirSea Battle, A Point of Departure Operational Concept," Center for Strategic and Budgetary Assessments (2010), 119-121, http://www.csbaonline.org/wp-content/uploads/2010/05/2010.05.18-AirSea-Battle.pdf (accessed 6 December 2012)

[84]Jan van Tol, et. al., "AirSea Battle," Center for Strategic and Budgetary Assessments, 18 May 2010, http://www.csbaonline.org/wp-content/uploads/2010/05/2010.05.18-AirSea-Battle-Slides.pdf (accessed 6 December 2012).

over the long term. The AirSea Battle concept ultimately endeavors to demonstrate U.S. capability and willingness to defend its allies and interests while denying a quick victory to the enemy.[85]

Major General Luo Yuan has expressed the concern of some Chinese strategists that the U.S. "pivot" to the Pacific is the manifestation of an U.S. strategy to contain China, not unlike the U.S.-led containment of the Soviet Union,[86] to wit: "the United States is making much of its 'return to Asia,' has been positioning pieces and forces on China's periphery, and the intent is very clear--this is aimed at China, to contain China."[87] Official U.S. government and government-sponsored documents argue for the necessity of crafting strategy that potentially constrains an aggressive China, while not being provocative towards a defensive China, and, if that fails, being able to defeat China's defenses. Thus, the region is caught between competing poles of China and the U.S., where both are committed to be "first among equals" in the region.

Secondary Source Materials: Independent Analysis

Sometimes, outsiders have the clearest view. An expert evaluation of various aspects of Chinese politics and culture can assist in properly framing and assessing the

---

[85]Ibid.

[86]Michael S. Chase, "Fear and Loathing in Beijing? Chinese Suspicion of U.S. Intentions," 30 September 2011, http://www.jamestown.org/uploads/media/cb_11_47.pdf (accessed 6 December 2012).

[87]Kathrin Hille, "US Seeks To Calm Beijing Containment Fears," *Financial Times,* 8 December 2011, http://www.ft.com/intl/cms/s/0/6f00abee-216f-11e1-a19f-00144feabdc0.html#axzz28kGsR1x7 (accessed 6 December 2012).

Chinese strategic outlook. All these materials ultimate provide clarity into some element of Chinese goals in the SCS.

China: A Country Study, is a report commissioned by the Library of Congress which articulates the evolution of certain Chinese foreign policy goals, specifically, "security, sovereignty and independence, territorial integrity and reunification, and economic development."[88] This report notes that, as one of the founding civilizations, China tend to view itself and its political interests at the center of the world-- "sinocentrism."[89] This report observes how China managed to preserve its core culture and even managed to assimilate its "barbarian" rivals, and explains how sinocentrism made possible China's ongoing manipulation of neighboring barbarian tribes to China's political and security benefit. This pragmatic technique of "using barbarians to control barbarians" continues to inform modern Chinese foreign policy.[90] Potentially, the Chinese wish to play various ASEAN nations off against one another with incentives in order to prevent a united front against Chinese claims in the SCS.

A Military History of China provides a very accessible overview of Chinese military history, and the authors argue that current Chinese military efforts are profoundly influenced by the aggregate effect of Chinese history and the influence of society. The

---

[88]Robert L. Worden, Andrea Matles Savada, and Ronald E. Dolan, ed., *China: A Country Study*, Federal Research Division, 1987, http://countrystudies.us/china/ (accessed 6 December 2012).

[89]Ibid.

[90]"Using barbarians to control barbarians" is a recurring theme in Chinese foreign policy, first employed by the imperialistic Han Dynasty Emperor Wu (ruled 141-87 BCE). See Sheng Ding, *The Dragon's Hidden Wings: How China Rises With Its Soft Power* (New York: Lexington Books 2008), 96. See generally, Federal Research Division, "China: A Country Study."

book argues the continuing focus of the Chinese military has remained very defensive over time, even as its military has modernized. The authors provide an overview of Chinese military operations since 1950, and in all cases noting how the Chinese were careful to couch their military actions as defensive and in protection of existing claims or borders.[91]

The book observes that Chinese military operations since 1950 have been limited campaigns in support of specific goals, usually the demarcation or claim of border territory. However, as circumscribed as these operations have been, China continues "to rely primarily on threats of force and coercion . . . it will not hesitate to use force in pursing its foreign policy ends."[92] The Chinese likely view operations in the SCS as defensive operations to retain rightful Chinese territory from historical foreign aggression.

China in the 21st Century: What Everyone Needs to Know provides a more broad-based view of the development and impact of current Chinese political views, and is a work of impressive clarity. *China in the 21st Century* might be described as "the view from Beijing" insofar as the author argues that the influences of nationalism, the media, the economy, and the Communist Party's views can only be properly understood from a Chinese perspective, and in this analysis, Chinese governance is ultimately adaptive and pragmatic.[93] This book argues that access to energy is one of the key concerns of the

---

[91]David Graff and Robin Higham, *A Military History of China* (Lexington: University Press of Kentucky, 2012), 37.

[92]Ibid., 282.

[93]Jeffery N. Wasserstrom, *China in the 21st Century; What Everyone Needs to Know* (New York: Oxford University Press, 2010), 127.

33

PRC's political leadership[94] with a compelling narrative of the potential importance of these SCS hydrocarbon resources and the long-term environmental effects of the PRC's transition from coal to natural gas. Such resources represent a prime future asset for a resource-hungry China.

The Party: The Secret World of China's Communist Rulers takes the reader inside the 73 million member Chinese Communist Party (CCP), among most important decision-making bodies in the world. Richard McGregor's[95] *The Party: The Secret World of China's Communist Rulers* is highly instructive on the inner workings of the CCP, depicting its byzantine structure and self-policing mechanisms to maintain control of power--particular power over the military. *The Party* relates the modern history of the PLA and its role in the PRC's governance and examines how the military, like much of the rest of Chinese society, has been forced to reform itself while retaining its loyalty to the CCP.

For example, *The Party* argues the army's initial reaction to the Tiananmen Square demonstrations was a watershed moment for the CCP, explaining how Lieutenant General Xu Qinxian--then Commander of China's 38th Army--refused to clear the square on verbal orders, leading to his arrest, incarceration, and expulsion from the party. This incident shocked the party leadership, forcing them to take additional measures to ensure the military's absolute loyalty in the future.[96] Among these measures was the creation of

---

[94]Energy, economy, environment, and endemic corruption being the four principal issues facing Chinese governance. Ibid., 127.

[95]McGregor was the former Chinese bureau chief for the U.K.-based *Financial Times* newspaper.

[96]James McGregor, *The Party* (New York: HarperCollins 2010), 117.

nearly 90,000 political cells within the PLA. The author observes that an independent

military presents a potential existential threat to the party. [97] Ultimately, *The Party*

represents a virtually insider account portraying the CCP as an organization of deep

secrecy, focused primarily on retaining power while maintaining its posture of distrust

and hostility towards the U.S.[98] Potentially, the rationale behind Chinese actions in the

SCS could be opaque and illogical to outside observers, so the U.S. should be prepared

for China to shift towards a more aggressive posture.

Interpreting China's Grand Strategy: Past, Present and Future is a RAND

Corporation study that proposes five consistent overarching Chinese goals; (1) "Efforts to

protect the Chinese heartland," (2) "Periodic expansion and contraction of periphery

control and regime boundaries," (3) "The frequent yet limited use of force against

external entities," (4) "A heavy reliance on non-coercive security strategies to control or

pacify the periphery when the state is relatively weak," and (5) "A strong, albeit sporadic,

susceptibility to the influence of domestic leadership politics."[99]

These five goals consistently drive a "realist" and "calculative" Chinese foreign

policy formulation--often at the same time. This study also predicts that China, consistent

with those five goals, likely intends to reclaim its place in the center of the world by

widening its sphere of influence and developing its military capabilities. The study

---

[97]Ibid., 112.

[98]Ibid., 110.

[99]Michael D. Swaine and Ashley J. Tellis, "Interpreting China's Grand Strategy: Past, Present, and Future," 2000, http://www.rand.org/pubs/monograph_reports/ MR1121.html p. 21 (accessed 6 December 2012).

further posits that--in the spectrum of outcomes between the dissolution of the PRC or an isolationist China--the most likely outcome is an assertive China.[100]

A review of a wide variety of secondary sources suggests that the U.S. must be prepared to face a resolute and assertive China that believes its sovereignty is being challenged.

The Anglo-American Gulf Engagement Strategy

While the geographic characteristics of the Persian Gulf and the SCS are distinct, the geopolitical considerations are similar. Both regions have global importance with respect to international trade, both share a complex security environment, and both feature smaller actors with shifting allegiances endeavoring to check local rivals and balance powerful outside forces; in the Pacific--China and the U.S., in the Gulf--the U.S.S.R., later Iraq and Iran.

In the Persian Gulf, the U.K. and the U.S. were effectively compelled into a unilateral regional policing function by the lack of a significant multilateral regional security treaty.[101] This is the case in the SCS region today. The similarities suggest that the Anglo-American Gulf engagement strategy could be a useful model for U.S. engagement in the South China Sea. A historical survey of the Anglo-American Gulf engagement is necessary to examine if such a case study could have applications to U.S. engagement in the South China Sea.

---

[100]Ibid., xii.

[101]With the notable exception of the Central Treaty Organization (CENTO), which, like SEATO, was dissolved in the wake of the Vietnam War by the late 1970s. The U.S. was never a signatory to CENTO, though it did participate and observe.

J. B. Kelly's[102] book *Arabia, the Gulf and the West* is the classic exploration of the history of British ends-ways-means strategy in the Persian Gulf. This text provides particular clarity on the strategic conditions of the mid-twentieth century Persian Gulf, and the author shows particularly keen insight in characterizing the political and security situation as the British influence waned. The book notes that regional conflict from within proved a bigger threat than without, and how sound policy balanced internal security issues created by indifferent local governance and the unpredictable political situation created by the Cold War.[103]

Kelly observes that the U.K., in providing for the security of Persian Gulf, was ever mindful that its power ultimately resided in its navy, so it made scant effort outside of the littoral states. Rather than investing large numbers of troops to prevent the consistent squabbles arising from the Gulf states' poorly demarked boundaries, the U.K. prudently restricted itself to protection against the Soviet Union and Iran.[104] Mindful that the Kremlin's favored mechanism to advance their foreign policy objectives was supporting insurgencies, the British generally supported the existing political structures of the Gulf nations.

The Politics and Security of the Gulf: Anglo-American Hegemony and the Shaping of a Region by Jeffery Macris provides a more updated study of the development of the dual hegemony of the U.S. and U.K. in the affairs of the Persian Gulf since the late

---

[102]Kelly served as an advisor to both the sheik of Abu Dhabi and sultan of Oman, and lectured at Oxford.

[103]The challenge presented by Oman is particularly illustrative. See J. B. Kelly, *Arabia, the Gulf, and the West* (New York: Basic Books 1980), 101-163.

[104]Ibid., 467.

nineteenth century, and chronicles the development of British investment in Persian Gulf security, which was then shared with, and later subsumed by the United States. Less a formal alliance and sometimes little more than a marriage of convenience, the U.K. and U.S. generally arrived at "gentlemen's agreements" that provided a united front. The wealthy U.S. provided hardware solutions to security problems while the U.K. relied on a longstanding official and semi-official network to provide manpower-focused solutions.[105] This book describes how a synergistic relationship developed between the rulers of the Persian Gulf, who needed security, and the outside powers, which needed their resources.[106]

For clarity into the back-story of the British protectorate of the littoral Gulf sheikdoms, *American Ascendance and British Retreat in the Persian Gulf Region* is unsurpassed. In many ways, this book is the last chapter of *Arabia, the Gulf and the West* except this book reaches the opposite conclusion--i.e., the British retreat from the Persian Gulf was probably inevitable.[107]

<u>Summary</u>

The similarity between the political realities in the twentieth century Persian Gulf and the developing situation in the SCS are striking. When analyzed properly, these insights can provide a window into prospective U.S. engagement strategies in the SCS.

---

[105]Ibid., 250-255.

[106]Jeffery Macris, *The Politics and Security of the Gulf; Anglo-American Hegemony and the Shaping of a Region* (New York: Routledge Press 2010), 257.

[107]W. Taylor Fain, *American Ascendance and British Retreat in the Persian Gulf Region* (New York: Palgrave MacMillian, 2008), 5.

The security situation in the Persian Gulf region saw a collection of small, militarily insignificant states facing a myriad of internal and external defense challenges. Over the twentieth century, the Anglo-American effort in the Persian Gulf allowed a slow but perceptible shift the defense burden from an outside responsibility of the Western powers to a shared effort.

CHAPTER 3

RESEARCH METHODOLOGY

<u>A Brief History of Anglo-American Gulf Engagement</u>

With the discovery of massive oil reserves in the Persian Gulf in the early

twentieth century--oil that would be required to power the Royal Navy--the U.K. could

no longer regard the Persian Gulf region as a mere secondary trade market for Indian

goods. While the Gulf was previously collateral to Britain's Indian interests, by the early

twentieth century, the Gulf was beginning to eclipse India in importance. The British

active policing function there began in the 1920s. In the wake of the First World War, the

U.K. had become the region's supreme outside power. The British were generally

unwilling to attempt to establish hegemony inland, but were willing to work through

existing tribal structure, as long as all parties understood the U.K.'s dominant role.

By the 1930s, the U.S. was present in the Persian Gulf in greater force--though a

far less pervasive influence than the British. The Second World War crystallized the U.S.

perspective of the Persian Gulf as a region of primary geo-strategic importance. The U.S.

initiated larger-scale trade and defense arrangements, particularly with Saudi Arabia,

laying the groundwork for a permanent U.S. military presence there.[108] By the end of the

Second World War, the U.S. force presence in the Gulf was yet greater, and the increased

security need put strategists to the task of crafting a workable regional policy. Later

developments such as the Cold War, the growth of Arab Nationalism, and the fallout

---

[108]Jeffery Macris, *The Politics and Security of the Gulf; Anglo-American Hegemony and the Shaping of a Region* (New York: Routledge Press 2010), 33-80.

from decolonization continually caused reevaluation and reconsideration of existing strategies.[109]

Beginning in the 1960s, advanced weapons systems were exported to the region (especially by the U.K.) including advanced fighter aircraft, modern armored vehicles, and, by the 1970s, modern naval vessels.[110] In addition to enhancing the local forces, both the U.K. and the U.S. maintained a robust personnel footprint and mentoring role within the militaries of friendly Gulf nations, often in direct support, advisory or even operational capacities. These relationships have proven effective and mutually beneficial.

For instance, the Royal Armed Forces of Oman is an increasingly professional armed force that, for five decades, has maintained very close relations with both the U.K. and U.S., which, in turn, permits Oman to secure the advanced military equipment and training it needs to effectively defend its vital strategic position.[111] Another example of long-term personnel support is the U.S. Military Training Mission to the Kingdom of Saudi Arabia, which has been operational since the Truman Administration, combining the efforts of direct U.S. military advisors and trainers with U.S. civilian contractors. The U.K. also maintains a robust training footprint in the kingdom, particularly within the Royal Saudi Air Force.

_____

[109]Ibid., 83-118.

[110]The U.K. exported English Electric "Lightning" fighters to Saudi Arabia beginning in 1965, with the first tranche coming directly from RAF stocks, manned by RAF pilots. The state-of-the-art British FV 4201 "Chieftain" tank was exported to Iran in the early 1970s. Jordan and Kuwait also received advanced arms from the U.K.

[111]Jane's Sentinel Security Assessment--The Gulf States, "Armed Forces (Oman)" 1 July 2011, http://articles.janes.com/articles/Janes-Sentinel-Security-Assessment-The-Gulf-States/Armed-forces-Oman.html (accessed 6 December 2012).

When post-WWII domestic fiscal exigencies caused the U.K. to withdrawal of the bulk of its Gulf forces, the militarily ascendant and economically secure U.S. took over the British role. In wake of the 1973 Oil Crisis, President Nixon signaled the United States' willingness to protect its oil supplies with military intervention even after Vietnam. By 1980, The Carter Doctrine stood for the proposition that outside control of the Persian Gulf was tantamount to an attack on vital U.S. national security interests.

Pursuant to these national security pronouncements, force requirements for defending U.S. Gulf interests went from a tertiary priority (*i.e.*, at European and Korean levels) to the highest priority. This reprioritizing led to in the creation of the Rapid Deployment Group, which eventually evolved, into The United States Central Command (USCENTCOM).[112] The Nixon and Carter regional policy priorities continued though subsequent presidencies, each administration appreciating the critical need to maintain the Gulf's *status quo*.

The 1970s oil revenue boom and the assertiveness of the U.S.S.R. drove large and ongoing Gulf states' arms purchases, and continues to place the region at the center of international weapons sales. The importance of the Persian Gulf's oil riches is self-evident, and after the Oil Crisis of the 1973, vitally important to the economies of Europe and North America, but also to developing Asian nations requiring petrochemical resources. Indeed, it was oil-fueled ships and petrochemical business interests that originally drove U.K. and U.S. defense interests into the Persian Gulf. From these shared interests, those two nations forged a workable model of regional deterrence and stability.

---

[112]U.S. Department of Defense, "U.S. Central Command History," http://www.centcom.mil/en/about-centcom/our-history/ (accessed 6 December 2012).

This Anglo-American Gulf engagement strategy furthered three principle goals: maintaining interstate order, protecting commercial interests, and excluding rival "great powers."[113]

This evolving U.S. strategy led to disasters (the fall of the Shah and the ascent of the Ayatollahs) and victories (the First Gulf War) in about equal measure. However, despite numerous interstate conflicts--including three of the largest wars since the Second World War (Iran-Iraq War, Operation Desert Storm, and Operation Iraqi Freedom)--the general borders of the region remain essentially as they were since the end of Ottoman rule. The Saudis, to name just one example, remain fiscally committed to their defense and bearing an important element of the defense burdens of the Gulf region. Illustrating this resolve, a recent Congressional Research Service report says the Saudi Arabia spent USD $33.7 billion on weapons in 2011--placing the kingdom among the world's biggest defense spenders.[114] Thus, it may be fairly stated that the Anglo-American effort to maintain the borders of the Persian Gulf region against both inside and outside players has been extremely successful.

Theater-Shaping Through Positioning, Personnel, and Procurement

The Anglo-American Gulf engagement strategy ultimately rested upon three points: (1) positioning, (2) personnel, and (3) procurement.

---

[113]Jeffery Macris, *The Politics and Security of the Gulf: Anglo-American Hegemony and the Shaping of a Region* (New York: Routledge Press 2010), 247.

[114]Richard A. Gremmet and Paul K. Kerr, "Conventional Arms Transfers to Developing Nations, 2004-2011," Congressional Research Service, 24 August 2012, http://www.fas.org/sgp/crs/weapons/R42678.pdf (accessed 6 December 2012).

1. Positioned regional forces were maintained at levels sufficient to deter aggression from within and without the Gulf.[115]

2. Personnel were made available to the Gulf states, in a variety of legal status such as secondment, direct deployment, and military contractors.

3. Procurement was made available to Gulf states, especially as their military forces and economies matured, providing mutual benefit to buyer and seller states.

Under this Anglo-American Gulf engagement strategy, nations jointly undertook substantial engineering and construction projects in furtherance of improving their combat power, like constructing permanent command posts and weapons systems installations, building modern sea- and airports, and refurbishing or installing civilian infrastructure.[116] These sorts of endeavors are referred to as "theater-shaping operations," a term-of-art for peacetime military engagement "designed to dissuade or deter adversaries and assure friends, as well as set conditions for the contingency plan and are generally conducted through security cooperation activities."[117] That is to say, shaping

---

[115]For both the U.S. and U.K., operations in the Gulf were of secondary importance to force requirements in Europe, and--for the U.S.--the Pacific.

[116]William Pagonis and Michael Krause, *Operational Logistics and the Gulf War*, Land Warfare Papers Series, No. 13, Institute of Land Warfare, Association of the United States Army, October 1992, http://www.dtic.mil/cgi-bin/GetTRDoc?AD=ADA278028 (accessed 6 December 2012).

[117]Office of the Chairman of the Joint Chiefs of Staff, Joint Publication 3-0, *Joint Operations*, 11 August 2011, v-8, http://www.dtic.mil/doctrine/new_pubs/jp3_0.pdf (accessed 6 December 2012).

operations are designed as peaceful dissuade-and-deter missions on behalf of allies, which simultaneously achieve goals that may assist in the prosecution of war.[118]

In summation, the current SCS situation may be concisely stated as: China will probably continue pursuing its "Nine Dotted Line" claims; ASEAN is likely the region's best local mechanism to check Chinese expansionism but currently lacks both the adequate military coalition infrastructure and diplomatic cooperation necessary to do so; and the U.S. continuing to focus on maintaining the status quo and deterring rival states from resorting to combat to settle boundary disputes.

This current SCS regional situation is meaningfully analogous to the underlying situation in the Anglo-American Gulf engagement model, which was highly effective in meeting the strategic ends of the U.S., U.K., and their allies. By deploying and embedding Western military personnel and military hardware, the U.K. and U.S. established and improved the regional powers' individual and collective defense capability. This alliance of great powers with regional powers was able to effectively deter most aggression, and capably fight when deterrence failed. Given these profound similarities to the current situation in the South China Sea region, this thesis uses the Anglo-American Gulf engagement strategy as a valid model to adapt and apply in furtherance of U.S. strategic goals to preserve the *status quo* in the region or further U.S. interests.

_____

[118]For example, a U.S. military engineering team that assists a host-nation engineering unit in the refurbishment of an airfield creates a more capable airfield for the host nation's military and improves civilian utility, while also increasing the airfield's prospective value as a strategic asset should the need arise.

CHAPTER 4

ANALYSIS

An assessment of potential Chinese Ends-Ways-Means in the SCS against the

history of the Anglo-American model of security engagement in the Persian Gulf region

yields three distinguishable mechanisms for potential U.S. regional engagement. Such

engagement mechanisms should focus on proper shaping to deter aggression. Should

deterrence fail, allow the best possible employment of U.S. and regional ally military

forces.

<u>Chinese Ends-Ways-Means in the South China Sea</u>

It can neither be argued nor ignored that China is undertaking a massive regional

military buildup and adding significant power projection capability in the South China

Sea. Threatening a potentially ruinous war against the U.S. is high-risk strategy, not

congruent with the typically pragmatic nature of Chinese political calculus.[119]

Perhaps the Chinese do not fully comprehend how their military posture is

inherently threatening to their neighbors, despite the fact they presume similar U.S.

postures are inherently malevolent. As Chinese strategic analyst Oriania Mastro noted, "I

have never heard a Chinese strategist admit that concern about China's rise is

---

[119]Michael D. Swaine and Ashley J. Tellis, "Interpreting China's Grand Strategy: Past, Present, and Future," 2000, http://www.rand.org/pubs/monograph_reports/ MR1121.html (accessed 6 December 2012).

understandable, that maybe other countries have a point in their critiques of Chinese behavior."[120]

Two Competing Views of Chinese Ends

Chinese "ends" typically fall into one of two major schools of thought: (1) Chinese strategic aims are essentially defensive in nature: deeply grounded in ancient Confucian principles such as filial piety, duty to family and community, cultivation of virtue and sincerity, and respect for Confucius' golden rule, "己所不欲，勿施於人" ("What you do not wish for yourself, do not do to others"). (2) Chinese strategic aims are essentially aggressive in nature; noting historic patterns of assertive and coercive behavior from the irredentist philosophy of the Han Dynasty to modern Chinese Socialist imperialism.[121]

It is conceivable that the PRC military buildup is simply an attempt to price the U.S. military out of the region. If this is true, the PLA already has significant overmatch against any individual regional power, and even all those regional powers collectively, assuming they were able to organize some military coalition. That power imbalance can become diplomatic leverage should Beijing persuade the regional powers that Washington may hold some interest in regional affairs, but in the event of hostilities, will be unwilling and unlikely to jeopardize American cities to defend the claims of far-away

---

[120]Oriana Skylar Mastro, "What's the truth about U.S.-China strategic mistrust? You can't handle the truth," *Foreign Policy*, 16 November 2012, http://ricks.foreign policy.com/posts/2012/11/16/whats_the_truth_about_us_china_strategic_mistrust_you_c ant_handle_the_truth (accessed 6 December 2012).

[121]Federal Research Division, "China: A Country Study," 127.

allies. That is to say, "Americans will not trade Los Angeles for Taipei."[122] Another

likely PRC strategy comes from the ancient Chinese scheme of "using barbarians to

control barbarians."[123] The U.S. presence in the SCS provides Beijing a certain assurance

the U.S. will prevent its regional allies from engaging in pointless or counterproductive

provocations. This hypothesis assumes a Chinese desire for a managing U.S. presence,

but only insofar as that presence is entirely defensive and accommodating of Chinese

policy, including, it must be presumed, "reunification" with Taiwan.[124]

The Carrot-and-Stick

The U.S. maintains a massive military presence in the Pacific. The forward

operating bases in Japan, the ROK, and Diego Garcia, plus large Pacific bases on Guam,

Alaska, and Hawaii are seen by Beijing as a purposeful check against Chinese

expansion.[125] To overcome this bar, the Chinese are investing heavily in controlling the

SCS: building significant facilities on Hainan Island, establishing bases in the Paracel

Islands, and making routine deployments to the Spratly Islands. Beijing views the U.S.'s

Pacific presence as the rival to their regional military superiority--except China's military

---

[122]Dalton Lin and Dave Ohls, "Nuclear Tiger with Paper Teeth: Putting China's Stagnant Nuclear Deterrent in International and Domestic Context" (Thesis, University of Wisconsin-Madison, 2008), 1, http://users.polisci.wisc.edu/klin/Lin&Ohls_china nukes.pdf (accessed 6 December 2012).

[123]See footnote 87.

[124]People's Liberation Army (Academy of Military Sciences, trans.), *The Science of Military Strategy,* ed. Peng Guangquian and Yao Youzhi (Beijing: Military Science Publishing House, 2005), 409.

[125]Kathrin Hille, "US Seeks To Calm Beijing Containment Fears," *Financial Times*, 8 December 2011, http://www.ft.com/intl/cms/s/0/6f00abee-216f-11e1-a19f-00144feabdc0.html#axzz28kGsR1x7 (accessed 6 December 2012).

buildup is well within its historical sphere of influence, while the Americans are simply unwelcome foreigners. Strategically, this could provide Beijing a carrot-and-stick approach.

The carrot: China persuades regional powers of their "us-against-the-foreigners" perspective, inspiring the regional powers to make some prompt accommodation with Beijing through bilateral negotiations--particularly if they come to believe that earlier agreements struck with the Beijing will be considerably more beneficial than later ones.

The stick: China engages in regional "Finlandization,"[126] a realpolitik strategy whereby smaller, less powerful countries attempt to preserve their sovereignty against superpower neighbors by simply choosing not to challenge the more powerful neighbor's hegemonic displays. Regional powers that resist bilateral negotiations with Beijing might simply be Finlandized into accepting China's definition of the region's political and military boundaries.

High-Tech Local War

Since the Second World War, Chinese strategists have been willing to graft certain Western innovations onto their vision of future Chinese strategy. These strategists predict that, because the risks of the exchange of nuclear weapons, future conflict will be localized, but otherwise high-intensity and relatively brief. Dubbed "high-tech local war," this innovative strategy means to allow Beijing to achieve positive, if limited, diplomatic objectives subsequent to military action at a relatively low cost.

---

[126]"Finlandization" is a term coined by West German political scientist Richard Löwenthal of the Free University of Berlin.

In a high-tech local war, the Chinese would pursue a limited military target with the ultimate purpose of securing a favorable negotiated settlement. Therefore, U.S. commanders should anticipate the PRC to engage in focused, incremental, military actions supported by high-tech information operations, followed by aggressive integrated diplomacy that threatens outside intervening actors, rather than expecting a massive Soviet-style assault.

Applying the Anglo-American Gulf Engagement Model to the SCS

The U.S. currently faces similar demands and pressures on its ability to rebalance to the Pacific. The Anglo-American Gulf engagement model discussed in Chapter 3 serves as a useful case study in effective regional engagement through application of a comprehensive theater-shaping approach. This approach was a triad of personnel, positioning of forces, and procurement--with the ultimate goal being to build the regional power's defense capabilities so they are individually and collectively better able to resist aggression.

Within the SCS region, the U.S. military already engages in a variety of small defensive deployments, presence patrols to ensure freedom of navigation, persistent personnel exchanges, and provides certain procurement opportunities to friendly states. With respect to the Anglo-American Gulf Engagement model's theater-shaping triad of personnel, positioning of forces, and procurement, a perfect balance of the three elements is the ideal, but not likely to be the reality. One element of the triad will axiomatically become the principle emphasis. Three possible courses of action (COA) emerge.

COA1: Positioning Emphasis--a surge strategy whereby the U.S. emphasizes its current *status quo* aggression-deterrence policies with an enhanced USN and USAF presence.

COA2: Personnel Emphasis--an embedded-personnel strategy whereby the U.S. deploy personnel to serve within a regional power's forces to (1) amplify their capabilities, (2) tailor procurement needs and train, and (3) assist in establishing a multinational defense collective.

COA3: Procurement Emphasis--a tripwire strategy whereby the U.S. commits a minimal U.S. force to the region which, in the event of hostilities, can provide an adequate response until a decisive force-response can be marshaled.

The three COAs are distinguished primarily by their emphasis on distinct elements of the Anglo-American Gulf Model. Courses of Action are measured by the "Feasible-Acceptable-Suitable-Complete-Distinguishable (F-A-S-C-D) metric. The element "completeness" shall herein be assumed by the follow-on planning requisite to execute any chosen COA. The remainder of the F-A-S-C-D metric will be applied to score each of the three COAs.

Analyzing COA1: Positioning Emphasis

A surge strategy whereby the U.S. emphasizes its current *status quo* aggression-deterrence policies with an enhanced USN and USAF presence. While the likelihood of SCS theater war is low, the potential costs of such a war are so high that deterrence should remain a central consideration of U.S. defense. The physical presence of combat-ready U.S. forces is a key element to the deterrence posture in the region..

51

Applying the Feasible-Acceptable-Suitable (F-A-S) analysis, this surge-strategy COA is very acceptable and highly suitable. This COA accommodates the traditional form of deterrence the U.S. and its allies and adversaries have long been accustomed to.[127] However, while this surge-strategy COA is highly acceptable and suitable from the military planner's standpoint, that opinion would probably not be shared by federal accountants.

Benefit

The clearest benefit of this strategy is that it represents a clear commitment backed by a powerful deterrent. It may be safely assumed that the synergies provided by "joint forces," including AirSea Battle, will continue as the preferred means of maximizing capabilities while minimizing expensive redundancies. The current demand for forces is determined by the USPACOM Commander who could make a compelling case for a greater resource commitment in the Pacific to provide continued robust U.S. deployments. These expanded deployments would make a powerful statement to U.S. friends and rivals about its commitments in the Pacific.

Liability

The liabilities of COA1 are its expense, its accommodation of "free riders,"[128] the invitation of higher risk of armed confrontation, and the limitation of overall flexibility

---

[127]The U.S. strategy of forward presence to avoid conflict is well-established, with U.S. forces being continuously forward-deployed since before World War II.

[128]As with U.S. security commitments to NATO, Washington continually complains that partners fail to pay their fair share (generally set at two percent of gross domestic product).

placed on the USPACOM commander. COA1 assumes the political willingness to prioritize increased SCS regional spending at the expense of other domestic and military priorities and must be considered in light of rather bleak economic realities. In an uncertain and even volatile economy, virtually all procurement programs face significant fiscal risk, so it may be safest to assume there may be no new materiel deployed, but the existing materiel may be redeployed.

The DoD procurement budget, $165 billion in 2008, is currently $108.5 billion[129]--a 34.25 percent decrease over four years. Given that eight of the ten most expensive defense procurement programs are exclusively USN (e.g., the Virginia class submarine and DDG-51 Aegis Destroyer), or USN-Joint programs (e.g., the F-35), the USN is uniquely exposed to additional DOD procurement budget cuts.

Operational deployment is a major cost-center within the USN budget. The more assets deployed, the more assets will need replaced or refitted. If an enhanced naval presence in the SCS is demanded pursuant to COA1, the increased expense of expanded operational deployment must come at the cost of other USN priorities, probably modernization and procurement.

COA1's enhanced forward presence would probably dampen regional powers' calls for protection, but will almost certainly exacerbate the U.S.'s "free-rider" problem. Further, COA1 probably also invites greater risk of direct confrontation with China due to increased USN and PLAN presence in the same space. While an armed confrontation is not in either party's best interest, history provides evidence how lock-in strategies and

---

[129]Barr Group Aerospace and J. Kasper Oestergaard, "U.S. DODDefense Spending," Aeroweb Defense Spending Database, http://www.bga-aeroweb.com/Defense-Spending.html (accessed 6 December 2012).

misperceptions of operational advantages can lead to excessively risky and ultimately self-defeating actions.[130] Finally, it is axiomatic that U.S. forces committed in the SCS are forces that unavailable elsewhere. COA1 encumbers the United States' ability to timely and meaningfully respond to exigencies beyond the SCS region. COA1 is desirable from a deterrent-continuity and force-ratio standpoint, but self-defeating in its detrimental collateral effects.

Analyzing COA 2: Personnel Emphasis

An embedded-personnel strategy whereby the U.S. deploys personnel to serve within a regional power's forces to (1) amplify their capabilities, (2) tailor procurement needs and train, and (3) assist in establishing a multinational defense collective. COA2 cultivates improved political relationships with regional partners to discern their strengths and weakness to better tailor answers to their individual procurement and training needs and their larger collective defense requirements, all while presenting a more benign posture less likely to provoke Chinese fears of encroachment or encirclement. Moreover, the sustained presence of U.S. personnel in a training and assistance role is very likely to produce positive effects for regional defense forces. In making those partner forces more effective, the overall security posture of the SCS can be increased in a cost-conscious and politically sensitive manner.

Applying a feasibility-acceptability-suitability analysis, the substantial investment of U.S. time and personnel, combined with the undetermined willingness of host-nation

---

[130]For example, the Japanese in 1941 and the North Koreans in 1950, both badly miscalculated the risk of engaging in armed conflict, and each overestimated their combat power advantages.

governments to facilitate the critical mass of personnel necessary to make this strategy successful, makes COA2's feasibility unclear. While probably acceptable to the U.S., COA2 might fail to represent the requisite investment to assure the regional powers of Washington's interest in ensuring regional stability. COA2 suitability relies upon the political success of committing U.S. personnel, rather than committing U.S. hardware.

Benefit

Chief among the advantages of COA 2 are its cost-effectiveness, efficiency, discreet and less antagonistic public profile. Because the SCS region has no effective multinational defense collective, regional powers have significant security holes, procurement redundancies, and a lack of a vision regarding their collective defense. In COA2, personnel should be selected with an eye toward their abilities to forge the types of relationships NATO has endeavored to create. However, NATO--despite five decades of defense-planning experience--continues to face significant hurdles in the execution of even limited military operations.[131]

COA2 requires selected personnel to spend large segments their career in the SCS region, pursuing a non-traditional officer career path, well outside the typical career-grading scheme.[132] By regionally aligning a cadre of personnel, the U.S. can develop a

---

[131]Kirk Volker, "Don't Call it a Comeback," *Foreign Policy*, 23 August 2011, http://www.foreignpolicy.com/articles/2011/08/23/dont_call_it_a_comeback (accessed 6 December 2012).

[132]For U.S. military officers, upward career progression is generally predicated on a variety of factors; performance evaluations, operational needs, etc. Officers are also and ranked by comparison with their peers. For a discussion of this issue viz. the army officers who face the dilemma of "officer career management" vs. "operational needs," see LTC Daniel E. Mouton, "The Army's Foreign Area Officer Program: To Wither or to

host of relationships with local governments to create a well of regional experience from which to draw during all operations. These officers would also be uniquely suited to help determine specific procurement solutions. This would be vastly preferable to the usual small-nation hodgepodge of mismatched equipment, disparate parts suppliers, and inconsistent training requirements that too often hobble small-nation militaries, diminishing their operational effectiveness. Moreover, increasing FMS can offset U.S. operational costs.

Some procurement efforts can helpfully function as theater-shaping operations. Infrastructure, however vulnerable, will be necessary for U.S. forces to effectively operate in theater. For instance, within the AirSea Battle framework, both the USN and USAF require aerial refueling tankers, which require large fixed airfields. As U.S. forces learned during the Gulf War, Saudi Arabia's mature infrastructure was crucial to deliver needed forces into theater. Similarly, the capacity of the Saudi military to effectively assist in the defense of transiting U.S. forces was also crucial. An analogous situation will surely arise in the event of hostilities in the SCS region. Through integrating procurement and infrastructure, total deterrence capability of all forces is enhanced while peacetime utility improves.

Pursuant to the Anglo-American Gulf engagement model, U.S. strategic goals in the SCS region may be met at comparatively low price through cost-shifting certain expenses to the regional states who, through strong and mutually beneficial politico-

---

Improve?" *Army,* March 2011, 21-24, http://www.ausa.org/publications/armymagazine/ archive/2011/3/Documents/FC_Mouton_0311.pdf (accessed 6 December 2012).

military relationships with the U.S., will become increasingly willing and able to shoulder their own defense burdens.

Liability

This course of action does have the inherent disadvantages of being a protracted process that pushes frontiers of the means by which U.S. military forces do their peacetime missions. In addition, without the investment of assets, all may read such a policy as indifference. Pursuant to COA2, a deeper understanding of each regional partner's security needs will require a greater investment of time and resources. The current security cooperation program, administered by the United States Security Assistance Organizations (SAOs)[133] is a starting point, but an engagement of much greater breadth and depth is fundamental and crucial to COA2's success.

While the U.S. does have an existing Personnel Exchange Program, it is quite limited in participation, scope, and duration. Other officers, such as attachés and foreign area officers, have limited operational roles and a challenging peacetime mission. These programs focus on engagement with foreign militaries rather than long-term integration. In the Pacific, most of these exchanges have been with Japanese or the ROK militaries.

There is little evidence that an *ad hoc* immersion program would provide any sort of useful wartime coordination function or otherwise bind a collection of co-belligerents into a more effective, unified force--but even an *ad hoc* immersion program, and nothing more, is preferable to the existing, but inadequate, DoD global rotational personnel

---

[133]The SAOs are focused on FMS and training, and are typically tasked with a number of additional missions beyond relationship-building. Both the Army Special Forces and the Department of State also have existing liaison missions, which like SAO, are very much in-demand yet extremely constrained in size.

strategies. Under the current personnel policy, assignments for military officers might have significant exposure to a region over a career or none at all. Institutionalizing regional experience is a nearly cost-neutral first step to creating expertise, but COA2's enhanced and embedded personnel deployment framework represents new frontiers.

COA2 assumes certain risks. The absence of continued presence of a substantial U.S. military hardware in the SCS region may invite Chinese forces to push harder, increasingly farther from their mainland borders. Because COA2 cultivates regional partners to take charge of their own defense both individually and via multinational defense collectives, there is some danger the strategy could be misinterpreted as an unwillingness to act as a reliable and resolute military and diplomatic ally. Put simply, the United State's willingness to place a large number of U.S. military personnel and equipment at risk on another's behalf sends the unambiguous statement, "The United States is inexorably committed to your security." Without that unambiguous statement, partner nations may come to believe the U.S. is willing to providing everything *except* the help they will actually need during armed conflict. Even more counterproductive, regional powers may come to believe that in the event of armed conflict, the U.S. military may choose to cross whatever face-saving "golden bridge" the Chinese offer.

COA2 must pay particular consideration to the United States' existing relationships, legal requirements, and treaty obligations with the ROK, Taiwan, and Japan, while balancing the considerations of the SCS and the Pacific region. Merely ramping up the U.S. military presence in the region is likely to be viewed by the Chinese as Washington's being aggressive or de-stabilizing. COA2's embedding strategy subtly downplays the provocation by framing additional U.S. forces as regional assistants rather than regional aggressors.

COA2 is profoundly more cost-effective than COA1, but may engender the misperception of the U.S. as a distant and disinterested ally, which could lead certain regional powers conceding to Beijing, or it may even invite China to proceed with consolidating its SCS claims without restraint. COA2 relies on substantial, well-placed, effective embedded personnel who can capably achieve their local objectives, which may actually prove sufficient to establish the U.S.'s genuine commitment to regional engagement--signaling traditionally accomplished by a massive show of force, without the expense and provocation.

Analyzing COA3: Procurement Emphasis

A tripwire strategy whereby the U.S. commits a minimal U.S. force to the region that, in the event of hostilities, can provide an adequate response until a decisive force-response can be marshaled. A tripwire force is sufficient to delay an aggressor until the bulk of the force arrives to deal with the aggressor decisively. COA3 prioritizes cost-effectiveness over presence, while it accepts that the bulk of U.S. Pacific military forces will be focused on other priorities. COA3 relies on the inherent mobility of air and naval forces within the AirSea Battle framework to answer regional aggression.

Applying the feasibility-acceptability-suitability analysis, COA3 has reasonable suitability. Even a token U.S. presence creates deterrent effect, and a tripwire force capable of defending itself would likely give pause to a rational actor. COA3's acceptability to U.S. policy-makers is high. COA3 does accept that multiple defense commitments require commanders to accept risk, and this risk, while high, is indistinct from the current regional situation.[134] However, given the tripwire force is likely the most easily defeated, COA3 has very low suitability.

Benefit

Attributes of this COA are primarily its thrift, and being visibly forward deployed for diplomatic purposes and ready for combat operations. COA3 contemplates the dual requirements of peacetime mobility and consistent deterrence, with due consideration to the burdensome logistics inherent in distant Pacific operations. COA3 demands a smaller and cost-conscious level of U.S. force commitment, positioning only the minimum forces necessary deter regional aggression. The qualitative advantage of U.S. forces against likely adversaries theoretically works in favor of COA3, but is contingent on whether the U.S. retains its qualitative advantage into the future.

Liability

This Course of Action has a definite historical weight against it, as similar employment has been a loser so far. In the present, such limited forces plays directly into Chinese "high-tech local war" strategy. Historically, a tripwire strategy in Asia is an unmitigated failure. In the 1920s and 1930s the grim realities of the Great Depression rendered the U.S.'s Asiatic fleet a poorly resourced tripwire force intended to do little more than delay Japan and buy time for the rest of the fleet to arrive; however, the Asiatic

---

[134]For example, Singapore's agreement to host four Littoral Combat Ships, probably at the existing U.S. Navy base at Sembawang. See Marcus Weisgerber, "Singapore will now host 4 littoral combat ships," *Navy Times,* 2 June 2012, http://www.navytimes.com/news/2012/06/navy-singapore-host-4-littoral-combat-ships-060212d/ (accessed 6 December 2012).

Fleet tripwire was unable to even slow the Japanese advance.[135] In the 1962 Indo-Chinese War, China executed a wide-scale yet brief assault, followed by a unilateral ceasefire and withdrawal. The conflict's short duration and limited objectives allowed the Chinese to preempt any slow-to-respond intervention by the U.S. and U.S.S.R; thus, the Chinese aggressors were able to set the conditions for a favorable peace, while cleverly framing international perceptions of Chinese legitimacy and restraint.[136]

More to the point, *The Science of Military Strategy's* "high-tech local war" is precisely the sort limited-duration Chinese strategy that addresses COA3. Any Chinese aggressor will be carefully scaled to overmatch its tripwire opponent, especially for the short duration. The PLA would probably execute a limited-duration war that inflicts substantial casualties, immediately followed by a unilateral cease-fire before the full might of the U.S. military arrives. This pause would allow the Chinese to publicly express hope for a negotiated solution, where China may achieve the legitimacy of a diplomatic victory despite its illegitimate aggression. Even this poor outcome is preferable to full-scale armed conflict, given the nuclear capabilities of China and the U.S. Generating the right balance of minimum effective deterrence is difficult, and likely only to become clear after its failure or success. COA3 accepts substantial risk for U.S.

---

[135]Jeffery Nelson, "ABDACOM: America's First Coalition Experience in World War II" (Master's Thesis, University of Kansas, 2012), http://krex.k-state.edu/dspace/bitstream/handle/2097/13618/JeffreyNelson2012.pdf?sequence=1 (accessed 6 December 2012).

[136]R. Swaminathan, "Lessons of 1962: A Stock Taking After 40 Years," South Asia Analysis Group, Paper 693, 20 May 2003, http://www.southasiaanalysis.org/%5Cpapers7%5Cpaper693.html (accessed 6 December 2012).

defeat and capitulation, while providing Beijing major diplomatic payoff for a minor military gambit.

Choosing the Right COA

Washington's and Beijing's objectives in the SCS region must be clearly understood to arrive at the appropriate COA. Washington's stated objectives are the maintenance of the political and security *status quo* alongside proving a dedicated commitment to maintaining an ongoing rapid-response military presence to deter armed conflict. Beijing's objectives are asserting its dominant regional role pursuant to their expansive regional territorial claims while resisting outsider meddling and aggression, and pursuing bilateral negotiations with regional states where the China retains the lopsided power advantage.

Optimally, the ideal COA would (a) support the U.S. objectives with a high level of U.S. involvement in the area without siphoning off the funds required for modernization and other operational exigencies, (b) work within the Pentagon's AirSea Battle framework, (c) demonstrate U.S. regional commitment to U.S. allies and partners, and (d) be politically sensitive to Chinese concerns about outsider meddling and aggression, while (e) being capable of addressing Chinese tactics from its known historical and current stated mechanism as shown by the 1962 India-China war's "aggress-withdraw-set terms" strategy to their innovative "high-tech local war" framework.

COA2 best balances and meets these criteria. This framework enables the support of U.S. national strategy as part of both the "pivot" or "rebalancing" of Asian-focus forces, embeds personnel within partner states' forces to amplify their capabilities, helps to focus and fill their particular procurement needs, and assists in creating a multinational defense collective, all while allowing the budgetary room for modernization and force recapitalization. COA2 accommodates the modernization and force recapitalization essential to the technology and force requirements inherent in the AirSea Battle framework, which allows for continuing effective deterrence of near-peer military forces. The stationing and exchange of substantial personnel with SCS regional partners via a program like AfPak Hands would demonstrate a visible long-term commitment. This structure allows for the infrastructure and allied forces necessary for the establishment of a successful defense collective in a most politically neutral fashion possible. Likewise, COA2's regional commitment is signaled in a manner least likely to provoke Chinese fears of U.S. aggression or containment. Ultimately, COA2 creates the conditions where, should regional aggression occur, the regional partners will be well-positioned to provide for both their individual and mutual defense.

All elements of the personnel-positioning-procurement triad were applied in the Persian Gulf context, as they would likely be in any prospective SCS scenario. However, one of the elements will necessarily be emphasized in any case. With respect to the SCS region, the emphasis on personnel provides the U.S. with the most effective regional engagement model.

CHAPTER 5

CONCLUSION AND RECOMMENDATIONS

The application of a personnel intensive posture in the SCS does require further

validation and study of other spin-off questions. A variety of diplomatic and political

issue should be explored to compliment nearly any policy for SCS engagement. In

addition, procurement, positioning, and personnel issues also require exploration and

review.

Diplomatic Recommendations

The SCS region has no analogous arms-control treaty to the U.S.-Russian Treaty

on Intermediate-Range Nuclear Forces (INF), nor any verification and monitoring efforts

analogous to Europe's Treaty on Open Skies,[137] which allows its signatory members the

mutual right of reconnaissance overflight. The only SCS regional powers that are official

partners in the Missile Technology Control Regime[138] are Australia, Japan, and the ROK,

leaving the region's proliferation of missile technology largely unabated.

The United States government must--as part of any COA--encourage the

establishment and expansion of appropriate regional arms control and security

---

[137]Beyond permitting the right of reconnaissance overflight, the Treaty on Open Skies also provides for the sharing among all members of any information thus collected by any member.

[138]"The Missile Technology Control Regime is an informal and voluntary association of countries which share the goals of non-proliferation of unmanned delivery systems capable of delivering weapons of mass destruction, and which seek to coordinate national export licensing efforts aimed at preventing their proliferation." See generally the official website of the Missile Technology Control Regime, http://www.mtcr.info/ english/partners.html (accessed 5 August 2012). It should be noted that the PRC, while not officially a partner, chooses to observe certain aspects of this regime.

agreements. For instance, the INF could be revisited and expanded. The INF was born

from the 1980s "arms race," that led to extensive proliferation of missiles in Europe.[139]

The parties subsequently agreed to the mutual elimination of their inventory of land-

based cruise and ballistic nuclear-capable missile systems with ranges between 350-3400

nautical miles (500-550 km).

Once a landmark arms-control treaty, the INF is not merely obsolete, it is

perversely counterproductive, given the proliferation of Chinese missile technology in the

ensuing decades. Indeed, China's SAC intermediate range missiles threaten both the U.S.

and Russian Federation, but neither party is able to field a specific counter to that Chinese

threat, due to the constraints of the INF. In answer, the Russian Federation and the U.S.

may choose to amend the INF to allow missiles previously banned under the agreement

to be deployed within the Pacific and SCS regions, while they continue to forbid their

deployment in Europe.[140] Another option might be to field missiles banned under the INF

in a manner similar to U.S.-NATO "weapons-sharing"; that is, banned weapons could be

---

[139]Originally the U.S. and U.S.S.R., now binding on the treaty's successor state, the Russian Federation.

[140]Mark Stokes and Dan Blumenthal, "Can a treaty contain China's missiles?" *Washington Post,* 2 January 2011, http://www.washingtonpost.com/wp-dyn/content/article/2010/12/31/AR2010123104108.html (accessed 6 December 2012).

deployed[141] subject to a collateral agreement between the nation who owns and controls the weapons, and the nation who is basing them.[142]

The lack of regional arms agreements does not cripple or defeat the embedded-personnel model. Treaty "workarounds" and collateral agreements may be the sort of stopgaps that could functionally accommodate any U.S. defense strategy model until substantial and effective regional arms control and security agreements can be achieved through diplomacy.

Political Recommendations

It is almost certain the PRC will treat as a provocation any effort to create new formal multilateral military alliances along the lines of NATO.[143] This political reality means the U.S. will have to rely on informal and bilateral agreements to grow a regional collective defense.

---

[141]The argument is that, should those weapons be required in the event of armed hostilities, the applicable UN Treaty on the Non-Proliferation of Nuclear Weapons (NPT) obligations would no longer be controlling. See Bruno Tertrais, "NATO and the Future of the NPT," Occasional Paper 21, Rome, ed. Joseph F. Pilat and David S. Yost, NATO Defense College, Academic Research Branch, May 2007, 92, http://www.ndc.nato.int download/downloads.php?icode=21 (accessed 6 December 2012).

[142]It is the position of the United States government that this sort of collateral agreement is in compliance with treaty obligations under the NPT because no actual transfer takes place as long as the U.S. retains control of the arms it bases elsewhere. See Hans M. Kristensen, "US Nuclear Weapons in Europe" (Natural Resources Defense Council presentation to the German Bundstag, 25 February 2005), http://www.nrdc.org/ nuclear/euro/euro.pdf (accessed 6 December 2012).

[143]You Ji, "Meeting the Challenge of Asia's Changing Security Environment: China's Response to the New Threats," National Institute of Defense Studies, 2011, http://www.nids.go.jp/english/publication/joint_research/series6/pdf/08.pdf (accessed 6 December 2012).

Noting that a robust institution like NATO continues to face operational challenges, it must be assumed that it will likewise take decades to forge an effective defense collective in the SCS region. A program like "AfPak Hands" may accelerate the process. In this type of program, selected officers, and non-commissioned officers would gain special expertise in local security issues through cultural immersion and extended service with partner nations.[144] Expanding the current Personnel Exchange Programs (PEP) and creating an "Asia-Pacific Hands" program (on the AfPak Hands model) in the pursuit of developing an effective regional multinational defense collective would be the logical first step in pursuing this strategy. Introducing NATO Standarization Agreements (STANAGS) to nations not currently using STANAGS personnel exchange programs should enhance operations and logistics interoperability with other regional powers.

Procurement Recommendations

The U.S. procurement community should develop export-focused procurement programs aimed at providing even technically unsophisticated nations the capability for modern armed forces at cost-points competitive even with rock-bottom arms dealers like Russia.

In adapting the Anglo-American Gulf engagement model, the focus should shift from expensive high-end programs born by the U.S., toward an approach that builds SCS regional partner's military capability in a cost-sensitive manner. Specifically, the U.S.

---

[144]Office of the Chairman of the Joint Chiefs of Staff, "AfPak Hands (APH) Project Overview," 26 August 2011, http://www.jcs.mil//content/files/2011-09/090811135844_AFPAK_Hands_Program_Brief.pdf (accessed 6 December 2012).

should pursue programs tailored to permit regional partners to address their individual defense shortfalls, with a mind toward functioning as part of a defense coalition.

Obviously these tailored procurement programs represent substantial investment and invite feasibility concerns. Cost-conscious and locally tailored FMS products must be developed to ensure functional interoperability. The specialized training permitted through personnel exchange considerably enhances functional product interoperability. A unified program of tailored FMS products and specialized training[145] would not only optimize the host nation's defense capabilities, it would enhance the region's collective defense response.

The aircraft that would likely meet these criteria would be a medium-lift aircraft between the C-130 and C-17, export of Generation 4+ fighters like the F-15, F-16, and F/A-18, and theater surface-to-air missiles like Patriot and Theater High Altitude Air Defense, with the latter's ability to defend again medium-range ballistic missiles being the critical capability. Floating assets that meet these criteria include a frigate-sized surface combatant, a diesel-electric submarine, and short-to-medium range surface-to-surface missiles.[146]

The study of the feasibility of creating actual procurement programs for maritime defense also needs study. Immediately, the likely programs would focus on sovereignty

---

[145]When American training comes as part of the "service after the sale," this manifestly benefits the purchasing nation, while the U.S. is assured of the purchaser's capability and interoperability.

[146]Production and fielding ground-based intermediate range missiles is currently limited by "The Treaty Between the United States of America and the Union of Soviet Socialist Republics on the Elimination of Their Intermediate-Range and Shorter-Range Missiles," colloquially The Intermediate-Range Nuclear Forces Treaty (INF).

patrol and policing within the maritime domain. Four key weapons systems would be air-to-air fighters, transport aircraft, surface sea combatants, and submarines. These weapons allow for airspace and sea policing, sea denial and delivery of ground forces. Ideally, these systems would be standardized U.S. equipment, or built to NATO STANAGS, to maximize interoperability with U.S. forces.

The history of successful export-focused weapons programs in the U.S. is limited. The most notable of these programs in the Cold War context was the F-5 fighter aircraft, which was originally a privately funded design that eventually achieved significant export success. The feasibility and desirability of continued export of existing Generation 4.5 fighters like the F-15, F-16, and F/A-18 series and associated targeting and weapons systems, should be studied for its impact on the continued development and fielding of U.S. systems and the U.S. industrial base. With regard to airlift capability, currently, the U.S. exports C-130 and C-17 cargo aircraft. While the C-17 is widely recognized as a preeminent strategic airlifter, its high acquisition costs and per hour flight costs render it unaffordable to many regional powers.[147] The Lockheed C-130 is likewise the gold standard in tactical airlifters, but faces some range and speed limitations. The Airbus A400 attempts to bridge this game, but is still in development. The evaluation of the advantages of an affordable operationally focused airlifter should be studied.

Similarly, any potential SSK submarine project must assess the impact of the project on the ability of U.S. industrial base to design, build, and sustain conventional

---

[147]USAF and National Science Foundation reporting suggests that (in 2008-dollars) it cost $240 million to acquire a C-17, plus roughly $12 thousand per flight hour.

submarine capability.[148] Although the U.S. has proposed FMS of conventional submarines to Taiwan as recently as 2001, a combination of Chinese pressure and U.S. technical difficulties has stymied deliveries. Recently, Taiwan has expressed interest in U.S. technical assistance for its indigenous submarine construction program.[149] Some other regional powers lack Taiwan's submarine knowledge and overall depth of technical capacity, and thus would require a turn-key submarine program. The history of the Collins-class SSK in Australian service should serve as a cautionary tale for the potential pitfalls facing a highly professional navy in the acquisition and operation of submarines. The maintenance requirements of modern systems, creation of trained crews and insatiable requirements of commanders once operational make a credible undersea deterrent a difficult proposition.[150]

While mildly less difficult than a submarine, procuring an effective yet affordable surface sea combatant is challenging. The logical candidate for FMS among the vessels built in the U.S. is the Littoral Combat Ship (LCS). However, this program of two competing ship types has been plagued with cost overruns and shrinking capability. If the LCS program matures, the likely fall in per unit costs will make the LCS a more desirable

---

[148]The James Martin Center for Nonproliferation Studies at the Monterey Institute of International Studies, "United States Submarine Import and Export Behavior," The Nuclear Threat Initiative, 9 August 2012, http://www.nti.org/analysis/articles/united-states-submarine-import-and-export-behavior/ (accessed 6 December 2012).

[149]Taipei Times, "Defense Ministry Lambasted Over Submarine Plans," 30 March 2012, http://www.taipeitimes.com/News/taiwan/archives/2012/03/30/2003529070 (accessed 6 December 2012).

[150]For a brief overview, see "Australia's Submarine Program in the Dock," *Defense Industry Daily,* 5 August 2012, http://www.defenseindustrydaily.com/Australias-Submarine-Program-In-the-Dock-06127/ (accessed 6 December 2012).

export program. One point in the LCS favor is its multi-role nature. The LCS design is intended to accept a variety of mission modules. When equipped with the proper mission modules, light amphibious, surface warfare, and anti-mine and anti-submarine warfare missions may be accomplished. For both the U.S. and foreign navies with limited budgets, a combination of existing multi-mission surface ship designs might be a better option.[151] For Asian navies, multi-mission frigates or destroyers, and amphibious shipping could represent a moderate priced and flexible capability.

While much of the hard data on weapons procurement remains proprietary to the manufacturers, the idea of creating affordable weapons systems for procurement is ultimately one with a significant history in the US. However, recent procurement programs have yielded very high-end programs competing on a crowded and highly competitive international arms sales landscape. The potential competitive benefit of "buying American" to allies should be the value-added of U.S. sourced equipment being combined with increased training and operational opportunities with U.S. forces. Such purchase, combined with long-term stationing of U.S. personnel on-board could provide a critical edge in such sales, thus maintaining the U.S. industrial base and furthering U.S. defense objectives.

<u>Positioning Recommendations</u>

Forward-based regional power forces should be prepared to act as wedges to allow U.S. and allied forces to enter the theater. While the U.S. has mature port facilities

---

[151]Paul Darling and Justin Lawlor, "Frigates for Streetfighters," *U.S. Naval Institute Proceedings* 137, no. 9 (September 2011), http://www.usni.org/magazines/proceedings/2011-09/frigates-streetfighters (accessed 6 December 2012).

in Singapore and historical ones in the Philippines, other bases should be aggressively explored and upgraded if necessary. A systematic hardening of such facilities would also be desirable, depending upon cost.

Personnel Recommendations

COA2 must be evaluated with due consideration to existing U.S. personnel policies. Existing U.S. military bureaucracy is poorly equipped to deal with either long-term stationing of personnel in the SCS region or the long-term integration of its personnel into foreign military services. Converting officers in dual-status as both reservists and contractors could be a workable solution within the existing legal and bureaucratic framework.

Currently, the officer-evaluation model is utterly inadequate for a flexible military with a local focus and global vision. The President's National Security Strategy recognizes the inherent value of personnel exchange, and the DoD needs to aggressively answer the requirement.

However, there is little research on the effect of PEP tours. PEP tours with other nations have to be career-positive for officers wishing to be retained on active duty. Ultimately, the DoD leadership should make the program a prime effort to attract the best officers into this role. However, until the Service Chiefs are convinced of the enhanced utility of an expanded PEP, for the individual officer selected for PEP, these tours are a career-limiting move regardless of how effectively the officer accomplishes U.S. strategic goals.

Currently, Personnel Exchange Program (PEP) tours are regarded as a "career-killers" due to the nature of the officer-evaluation process. In the typical career-

72

progression model, a superior officer evaluates subordinates and rank-orders them by performance. In these PEP situations, the evaluating officer is not a member of the U.S. military, and the U.S. officer being evaluated is not being compared to his or her peers within the U.S. military establishment. In short, this is not a meaningful comparison.

However, PEP tours must be evaluated on their own terms, relative to the particular circumstances, and based upon how well the officer furthers U.S. strategic goals. The current officer evaluation system would require modification of promotion criteria to properly weigh the theater-wide impact that PEP tours create. Instead of being one among a field, officers would be rated with respect to achievement of U.S. strategic goals within a specific regional power's context. Each PEP tour should have meaningful goals to make these tours at least neutral with respect to individual officer's career goals. Ideally, these tours should be tailored to produce career-furthering effects for those officers willing to make the greater sacrifice. Making PEP tours career-furthering creates incentives to attract the best-suited officers who are likely produce the best results. Within the existing U.S. military career-progression structure, this goal cannot be achieved.

The U.S. should encourage an expanded exchange of officers and senior enlisted between all branches of service, logically beginning with close allies Australia and New Zealand. After the U.S.'s foreign secondment program has matured, it could be offered to other partner and prospective-partner nations. The existing U.S. DoD National Guard State Partnership Program could also be expanded to include additional training opportunities for new sorts of personnel exchange. The inherent flexibility of the reserve component personnel would also function as an enormous asset. This sort of homegrown foreign secondment program--particularly in its broadest iteration--would necessarily go far to fill the United States' critical and persistent foreign-language-capability gap.

The uniquely British custom of foreign secondment--where individuals are detached from one nation's military for a long term in an allied service--merits additional scrutiny. Secondment differs from exchange tours mostly with respect to longevity. Secondment is at least a multi-year process which implies severing control of the originating nation over the officer.[152] Foreign secondment should be explored by the U.S. military as a strategy to build stronger military-to-military ties and to forge key personal relationships exceeding those which can be struck through ordinary bilateral military training.[153]

Conclusion

In the Persian Gulf region, the U.S. and U.K. used a triad of personnel engagement, positioning of moderate forces, and procurement to effectively build-up the self-defense capability of regional powers. Despite resource constraints and a dangerous situation in the Gulf, the U.S. and U.K. were able to stabilize a region presenting a wide

---

[152]While officers in such cases usually resign, the agreement usually has mechanisms to return to one's home countries, or even the service, without significant obstacles. Such agreements were made with Americans who joined the American Volunteer Group in China before the U.S. entry into World War II. One country essentially loans officers and/or technical experts to another country's military. Secondment officers are not mercenaries because they are commissioned into standing and recognized armed forces.

[153]For an example of seconded officers in the Persian Gulf, see Jeffery Macris, *The Politics and Security of the Gulf; Anglo-American Hegemony and the Shaping of a Region* (New York: Routledge Press, 2010), 134.

spectrum of defense challenges. The U.S. should regard its engagement in the Persian Gulf region as a model for future engagements in the SCS region.

As the United States embarks on its second century of sustained commitment of military forces to the SCS, questions of the proper mechanisms of regional engagement must be addressed. Once the U.S. was required to station forces, and little more. However, the geopolitical realities and national policies of all regional players have evolved, with the U.S. being no exception. The rise of Chinese political, military, and economic power must be addressed by the U.S. in concert with regional allies and partners, in a way that engages all participants in a positive or at least neutral manner.

ILLUSTRATIONS

2012).

Competing Claims in the South China Sea

Source: CIA Maps and Publications for the Public, "Competing Claims in the South China Sea," Energy Information Agency website, http://www.eia.gov/cabs/ South_China_Sea/Full.html (accessed 12 December 2012).

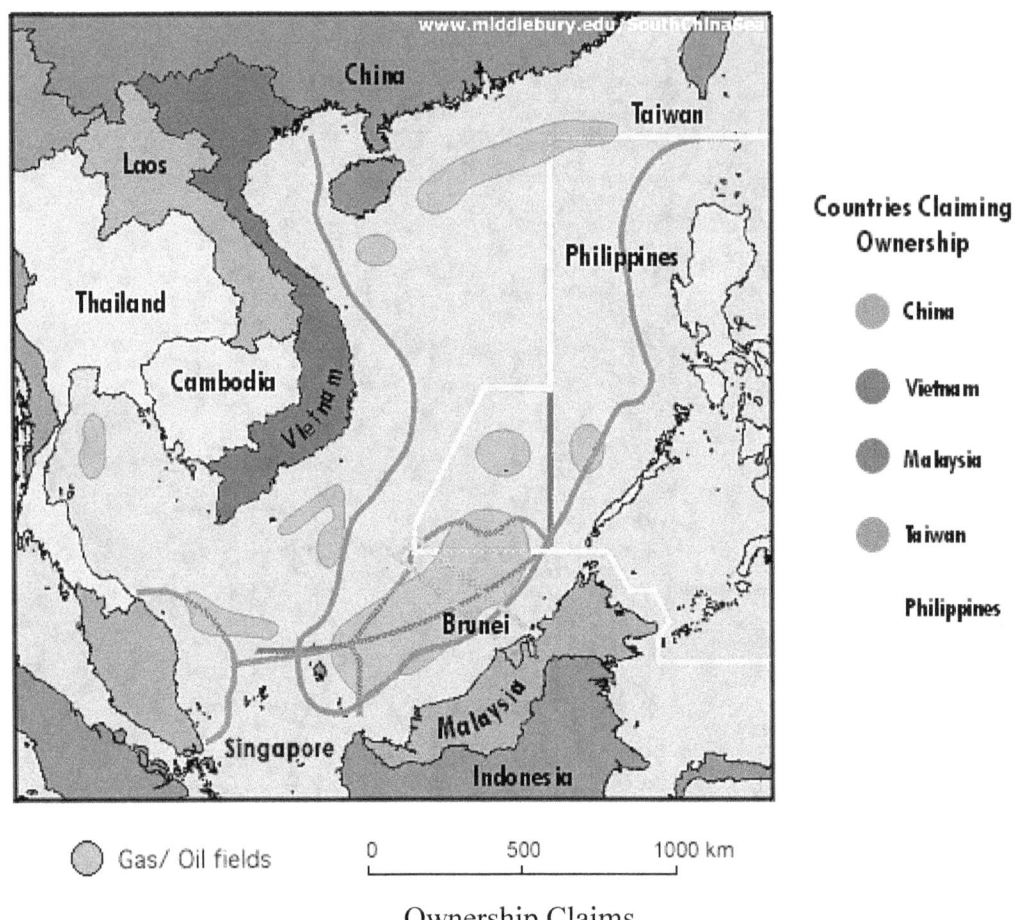

Ownership Claims

Source: Department of Energy, "Map of Competing Claims," Energy Information Agency website, http://www.eia.gov/EMEU/cabs/South_China_Sea/images/Ownership_Claims-Middlebury.gif (accessed 12 December 2012).

BIBLIOGRAPHY

Agence-Press France. *Asean Urged To Unite Over South China Sea.* 14 August 2012. http://bruneiembassy.be/asean-urged-to-unite-over-south-china-sea/ (accessed 6 December 2012).

Allen. Kenneth and Emma Kelly. "Assessing the Growing PLA Air Force Foreign Relations Program." *China Brief* 12, no. 9. (26 April 2012). http://www.jamestown.org/single/?no_cache=1&tx_ttnews%5Btt_news%5D=393 04 (accessed 6 December 2012).

ASEAN official charter. http://www.asean.org/archive/publications/ASEAN-Charter.pdf (accessed 6 December 2012).

Barr Group Aerospace, and J. Kasper Oestergaard. "U.S. DOD Defense Spending." Aeroweb Defense Spending Database. http://www.bga-aeroweb.com/Defense-Spending.html (accessed 6 December 2012).

Berteau, David J., and Michael J. Green. *U.S. Force Posture Strategy in the Asia Pacific Region: An Independent Assessment.* Center for Strategic and International Studies. August 2012. htp://csis.org/files/publication/120814_FINAL_PACOM_optimized.pdf (accessed 6 December 2012).

Bristow, Damon. "The Five Power Defence Arrangements: Southeast Asia's Unknown Regional Security Organization." *Contemporary Southeast Asia: A Journal of International and Strategic Affairs* 27, no. 1 (2005): 1-20.

British Broadcasting Corporation. "Leon Panetta: US to Deploy 60% of Navy Fleet to Pacific." 1 June 2012. http://www.bbc.co.uk/news/world-us-canada-18305750 (accessed 6 December 2012).

Chang, Amy, and John Dotson. "Indigenous Weapons Development in China's Military Development." U.S.–China Economic and Security Review Commission Staff Research Report, 5 April 2012. http://www.uscc.gov/researchpapers/2012/China-Indigenous-Military-Developments-Final-Draft-03-April2012.pdf (accessed 6 December 2012).

Chairman, Joint Chiefs of Staff. *AfPak Hands (APH) Project Overview.* 26 August 2011. http://www.jcs.mil//content/files/2011-09/090811135844_AFPAK_Hands_Program_Brief.pdf (accessed 6 December 2012).

———. Joint Publication, *Joint Operations.* 11 August 2011. http://www.dtic.mil/doctrine/new_pubs/jp3_0.pdf (accessed 6 December 2012).

Chase, Micheal S. "Fear and Loathing in Beijing? Chinese Suspicion of U.S. Intentions." 30 September 2011. http://www.jamestown.org/uploads/media/cb_11_47.pdf (accessed 6 December 2012).

Clinton, Hillary. "America's Pacific Century." *Foreign Policy*, November 2011. http://www.foreignpolicy.com/articles/2011/10/11/americas_pacific_century?page=ful (accessed 6 December 2012).

Cordesman, Anthony H., and Robert M. Shelala II. *The FY2013 Defense Budget. the Threat of Defense Cuts and Sequestration and the Strategy-Reality Gap.* Center for International and Strategic Studies. 12 June 2012. http://csis.org/publication/fy2013-defense-budget-and-new-strategy-reality-gap-0 (accessed 6 December 2012).

Darling, Paul, and Justin Lawlor. "Frigates for Streetfighters." *U.S. Naval Institute Proceedings* 137, no.9 (September 2011). http://www.usni.org/magazines/proceedings/2011-09/frigates-streetfighters (accessed 6 December 2012).

———. "Married to Clausewitz, but Sleeping with Jomini, How Operational Concepts Masquerade as Strategy, and Why They Must." *Infinity Journal* 2, no. 3 (Summer 2012): 21-24.

Defense Industry Daily. "Australia's Submarine Program in the Dock." 5 August 2012. http://www.defenseindustrydaily.com/Australias-Submarine-Program-In-the-Dock-06127/ (accessed 6 December 2012).

Department of the Navy. *Cooperative Strategy for 21st Century Seapower*. October 2007. http://www.navy.mil/maritime/Maritimestrategy.pdf (accessed 6 December 2012).

de Swielande, Struye. "The Reassertation of the United States in the Asia-Pacific Region" *Parameters* (Spring 2012). http://www.carlisle.army.mil/USAWC/parameters/Articles/2012spring/Struye_de_Swielande.pdf (accessed 6 December 2012).

Ding, Sheng. *The Dragon's Hidden Wings: How China Rises With Its Soft Power*. New York: Lexington Books, 2008.

The Economist. "Shopping Spree." 24 March 2012. http://www.economist.com/node/21551056 (accessed 6 December 2012).

Fain, W. Taylor. *American Ascendance and British Retreat in the Persian Gulf Region*. New York: Palgrave MacMillian, 2008.

Graff, David, and Robin Higham. *A Military History of China*. 2nd ed. Lexington, KY: University Press of Kentucky, 2012.

Gremmet, Richard A., and Paul K. Kerr. *Conventional Arms Transfers to Developing Nations, 2004-2011*. Congressional Research Service. 24 August 2012. http://www.fas.org/sgp/crs/weapons/R42678.pdf (accessed 6 December 2012).

Gutierrez, Jason. "Philippines sees Subic port as vital to US interests." *Agence-Press France*, 8 October 2012. http://www.abs-cbnnews.com/global-filipino/world/10/08/12/philippines-sees-subic-port-vital-us-interests (accessed 6 December 2012).

Hille, Kathrin. "US Seeks To Calm Beijing Containment Fears." *Financial Times*, 8 December 2011. http://www.ft.com/intl/cms/s/0/6f00abee-216f-11e1-a19f-00144feabdc0.html#axzz28kGsR1x7 (accessed 6 December 2012).

Indian Express. "Chinese warship confronts Indian Navy vessel in disputed zone: report." 1 September 2011. http://www.financialexpress.com/news/chinese-warship-confronts-indian-navy-vessel-in-disputed-zone-report/840151 (accessed 6 December 2012).

Information Office of the State Council of the People's Republic of China. *China's National Defense in 2010*. 31 March 2011. http://www.china.org.cn/government/whitepaper/node_7114675.htm (accessed 6 December 2012).

The James Martin Center for Nonproliferation Studies at the Monterey Institute of International Studies. *United States Submarine Import and Export Behavior*. 9 August 2012. http://www.nti.org/analysis/articles/united-states-submarine-import-and-export-behavior/ (accessed 6 December 2012).

Jane's Sentinel Security Assessment--The Gulf States. *Armed Forces (Oman)*. 1 July 2011. http://articles.janes.com/articles/Janes-Sentinel-Security-Assessment-The-Gulf-States/Armed-forces-Oman.html (accessed 6 December 2012).

Ji. You. *Meeting the Challenge of Asia's Changing Security Environment: China's Response to the New Threats*. National Institute of Defense Studies. 2011. http://www.nids.go.jp/english/publication/joint_research/series6/pdf/08.pdf (accessed 6 December 2012).

Jisi, Wang. *Multipolarity Versus Hegemonism: Chinese Views of International Politics*. China Institute of Science and Management. 28 September 2008. www.cssm.gov.cn/view.php?id=21083 (accessed 6 December 2012).

Kan, Shirley A. *China/Taiwan: Evolution of the One China Policy--Key Statements from Washington, Beijing, and Taipei*. Congressional Research Service. 24 June 2011. http://www.fas.org/sgp/crs/row/RL30341.pdf (accessed 6 December 2012).

Karber, Phillip A.. *Strategic Implications of China's Underground Great Wall*. Georgetown University. 26 September 2011. http://www.fas.org/nuke/

guide/china/Karber_UndergroundFacilities-Full_2011_reduced.pdf (accessed 6 December 2012).

Katusmoto, Hana. "U.S., Japan sign new five-year 'host nation support' agreement." *Stars and Stripes,* 21 January 2011. http://www.stripes.com/news/pacific/japan/u-s-japan-sign-new-five-year-host-nation-support-agreement-1.1324281 (accessed 6 December 2012).

Keating, Joshua. "U.S. reopening World War II bases in Pacific." *Foreign Policy,* 5 June 2012. http://blog.foreignpolicy.com/posts/2012/06/05/us_reopening_world_war_ii_bases_in_pacific (accessed 6 December 2012).

Kelly, J. B. *Arabia, the Gulf, and the West.* New York: Basic Books, 1980.

Kelso, T. S. "Analysis of the 2007 Chinese ASAT Test and the Impact of its Debris on the Space Environment." Technical Papers of the 2007 Advanced Maui Optical and Space Surveillance (AMOS) Technological Conference. Maui 2007. http://www.centerforspace.com/downloads/files/pubs/AMOS-2007.pdf (accessed 6 December 2012).

Khoo, Nicholas. "Breaking the Ring of Encirclement: The Sino-Soviet Rift and Chinese Policy toward Vietnam. 1964–1968." *Journal of Cold War Studies* 12, no. 1 (Winter 2010): 3-42.

Kiselycznyk, Michael, and Phillip C. Saunders. *Civil-Military Relations in China: Assessing the PLA's Role in Elite Politics.* National Defense University. August 2010. http://www.ndu.edu/press/lib/pdf/china-perspectives/ChinaPerspectives-2.pdf (accessed 6 December 2012).

Kristensen, Hans M. "New Chinese SSBN Deploys to Hainan Island." Federation of American Scientists. 24 April 2008. http://www.fas.org/blog/ssp/2008/04/new-chinese-ssbn-deploys-to-hainan-island-naval-base.php (accessed 6 December 2012).

———. "U.S. Nuclear Weapons in Europe." A Natural Resources Defense Council presentation to the German Bundstag. 25 February 2005. http://www.nrdc.org/nuclear/euro/euro.pdf (accessed 6 December 2012).

Langfitt, Frank. *America's Asian Allies Question Its Staying Power.* National Public Radio. 22 October 2012. http://m.npr.org/story/163378356 (accessed 6 December 2012).

Lin, Dalton, and Dave Ohls. "Nuclear Tiger with Paper Teeth: Putting China's Stagnant Nuclear Deterrent in International and Domestic Context." Thesis, University of Wisconsin-Madison, 2008. http://users.polisci.wisc.edu/klin/Lin&Ohls_china nukes.pdf (accessed 6 December 2012).

Lüthi, Lorenz M. "Beyond Betrayal: Beijing, Moscow, and the Paris Negotiations. 1971–1973." *Journal of Cold War Studies* 11, no. 1 (Winter 2009): 57-107.

Macris, Jeffery. *The Politics and Security of the Gulf; Anglo-American Hegemony and the Shaping of a Region.* New York: Routledge Press. 2010.

Mastro, Oriana Skylar. "What's the truth about U.S.-China strategic mistrust? You can't handle the truth." *Foreign Policy*, 16 November 2012. http://ricks.foreign policy.com/posts/2012/11/16/whats_the_truth_about_us_china_strategic_mistrust _you_cant_handle_the_truth (accessed 6 December 2012).

McGregor, James. *The Party.* New York: HarperCollins, 2010.

Miles, Donna. "Locklear: PACOM's Priorities Reflect New Strategic Guidance." *American Forces Press Service*, 12 May 2012. www.defense.gov/news/ newsarticle.aspx?id=116397 (accessed 6 December 2012).

Missile Technology Control Regime. http://www.mtcr.info/english/partners.html (accessed 5 August 2012).

Moss, Trefor. "Indonesian Military Powers Up." *The Diplomat*, 18 January 2012. http://thediplomat.com/flashpoints-blog/2012/01/18/indonesia-military-powers-up/ (accessed 6 December 2012).

Mouton, Daniel E. "The Army's Foreign Area Officer Program: To Wither or to Improve?" *Army Magazine,* March 2011. http://www.ausa.org/ publications/armymagazine/archive/2011/3/Documents/FC_Mouton_0311.pdf (accessed 6 December 2012).

Nabbs-Keller, Greta. "The Strategic Implications of of Closer China-Indonesia Relations." *Security Challenges* 7, no. 1 (2011): 23-41. www.securitychallenges. org.au/ArticlePDFs/vol7no3Nabbs-Keller.pdf (accessed 6 December 2012).

Nelson, Jeffery. "ABDACOM: America's First Coalition Experience in World War II." Thesis, University of Kansas, 2012. http://krex.k-state.edu/dspace/bitstream/ handle/2097/13618/JeffreyNelson2012.pdf?sequence=1 (accessed 6 December 2012).

Nong, Hong. *Interpreting the U-shape Line in the South China Sea.* China-US Focus, 15 May 2012. http://www.chinausfocus.com/peace-security/interpreting-the-u-shape-line-in-the-south-china-sea/ (accessed 6 December 2012).

Nuclear Threat Initiative. *Country Overview: China.* November 2012. http://www.nti.org/country-profiles/china/ (accessed 6 December 2012).

O'Rourke, Ronald. *Maritime Territorial and Exclusive Economic Zone (EEZ) Disputes Involving China: Issues for Congress.* Congressional Research Service. 22

October 2012. http://www.fas.org/sgp/crs/row/R42784.pdf (accessed 6 December 2012).

Pagonis, William, and Micheal Krause. *Operational Logistics and the Gulf War.* Land Warfare Papers Series. No. 13, Institute of Land Warfare, Association of the United States Army, October 1992. http://www.dtic.mil/cgi-bin/ GetTRDoc?AD=ADA278028 (accessed 6 December 2012).

Panetta, Leon E. "Shangri-La Security Dialogue." Speech presented at the Shangri-La Hotel, Singapore, 2 June 2012. Department of Defense. http://www.defense. gov/Speeches/Speech.aspx?SpeechID=1681 (accessed 6 December 2012).

Parameswaran, Prashanth. "The Limits to Sino-Indonesian Relations." *China Brief* 12, no. 8. (12 April 2012). http://www.jamestown.org/uploads/media/cb_04_02.pdf (accessed 6 December 2012).

People's Liberation Army (Academy of Military Sciences, trans.). *The Science of Military Strategy.* ed. Peng Guangquian and Yao Youzhi. Beijing: Military Science Publishing House 2005.

Pham, Derek. "On to the Hard Stuff: An ASEAN Defense Community?" Center for Strategic and International Studies. 9 May 2011. http://cogitasia.com/on-to-the-hard-stuff-an-asean-defense-community/ (accessed 6 December 2012).

President of the United States. *National Security Strategy.* May 2010. http://www.whitehouse.gov/sites/default/files/rss_viewer/national_security_strate gy.pdf (accessed 6 December 2012).

Secretary of Defense. *Annual Report to Congress: Military and Security Developments Involving the People's Republic of China 2012.* May 2012. http://www.defense.gov/pubs/pdfs/2012_CMPR_Final.pdf (accessed 6 December 2012).

Stokes, Mark, and Dan Blumenthal. "Can a treaty contain China's missiles?" *Washington Post.* 2 January 2011. http://www.washingtonpost.com/wp-dyn/content/ article/2010/12/31/AR2010123104108.html (accessed 6 December 2012).

Stokes, Mark. "China's Evolving Conventional Strategic Strike Capability." *Project 2049 Institute,* 14 September 2009, http://project2049.net/documents/chinese_ anti_ship_ballistic_missile_asbm.pdf (accessed 6 December 2012).

Swaine, Michael D., and Ashley J. Tellis. *Interpreting China's Grand Strategy: Past, Present, and Future.* RAND Corporation. 2000. http://www.rand.org/ pubs/monograph_reports/MR1121.html (accessed 6 December 2012).

Swaminathan, R. *Lessons of 1962: A Stock Taking After 40 Years.* South Asia Analysis Group. Paper 693. 20 May 2003. http://www.southasiaanalysis.org/%5Cpapers7%5Cpaper693.html (accessed 6 December 2012).

Taipei Times. "Defense Ministry Lambasted Over Submarine Plans." 30 March 2012. http://www.taipeitimes.com/News/taiwan/archives/2012/03/30/2003529070 (accessed 6 December 2012).

Tertrais, Bruno. *NATO and the Future of the NPT*. Occasional Paper 21. NATO Defense College, Academic Research Branch. Rome, May 2007. http://www.ndc.nato.int/download/downloads.php?icode=21 (accessed 6 December 2012).

Thayer, Carlyle A. "ASEAN'S Code of Conduct in the South China Sea: A Litmus Test for Community-Building?" *Asia-Pacific Journal*. http://www.japanfocus.org/-Carlyle_A_-Thayer/3813 (accessed 6 December 2012).

Thomas, Tim. "The Chinese Military's Strategic Mindset." *Military Review* (November-December 2007): 47. http://www.au.af.mil/au/awc/awcgate/milreview/thomas_china_mind-set.pdf (accessed 6 December 2012).

U.S. Central Command. "U.S. Central Command History." http://www.centcom.mil/en/about-centcom/our-history/ (accessed 6 December 2012).

U.S. Department of Defense. *National Military Strategy of the U.S. 2011.* http://www.jcs.mil//content/files/2011-02/020811084800_2011_NMS_-_08_FEB_2011.pdf (accessed 6 December 2012).

————. *Sustaining U.S. Global Leadership: Priorities for 21st Century Defense.* January 2012. www.defense.gov/news/Defense_Strategic_Guidance.pdf (accessed 6 December 2012).

U.S. Energy Information Administration. *South China Sea.* Country Analysis Briefs. March 2008. http://www.eia.gov/EMEU/cabs/South_China_Sea/pdf.pdf (accessed 6 December 2012).

U.S. Pacific Command. "About Us." http://www.pacom.mil/ (accessed 6 December 2012).

————. "USPACOM Facts." http://www.pacom.mil/about-uspacom/facts.shtml (accessed 6 December 2012).

van Tol, Jan. et. al. *AirSea Battle*. Presentation: Center for Strategic and Budgetary Assessments, 18 May 2010. http://www.csbaonline.org/wp-content/uploads/2010/05/2010.05.18-AirSea-Battle-Slides.pdf (accessed 6 December 2012).

―――. AirSea Battle. *A Point of Departure Operational Concept.* Center for Strategic and Budgetary Assessments. 18 May 2010. http://www.csbaonline.org/wp-content/uploads/2010/05/2010.05.18-AirSea-Battle.pdf (accessed 6 December 2012).

Volker, Kirk. "Don't Call it a Comeback." *Foreign Policy,* 23 August 2011. http://www.foreignpolicy.com/articles/2011/08/23/dont_call_it_a_comeback (accessed 6 December 2012).

Wasserstrom, Jeffery N. *China in the 21st Century; What Everyone Needs to Know.* New York: Oxford University Press, 2010.

Weisgerber, Marcus. "Singapore will now host 4 littoral combat ships." *Navy Times.* 2 June 2012. http://www.navytimes.com/news/2012/06/navy-singapore-host-4-littoral-combat-ships-060212d/ (accessed 6 December 2012).

Willard, Robert. ADM USN. *United States Pacific Command Strategic Guidance.* United States Pacific Command. http://www.pacom.mil/about-uspacom/strategic-guidance.shtml (accessed 6 December 2012).

Worden, Robert L., Andrea Matles Savada, and Ronald E. Dolan, ed. *China: A Country Study.* Library of Congress Federal Research Division, 1987. http://countrystudies.us/china/ (accessed 6 December 2012).

Yap. D. J. "Aquino to US: Speak up on West PH Sea." *Phillipine Daily Inquirer*, 20 November 2012. http://globalnation.inquirer.net/57120/aquino-to-us-speak-up-on-west-ph-sea (accessed 6 December 2012).

Zhang, Xiaoming. "China's 1979 War with Vietnam: A Reassessment." *The China Quarterly* 184 (December 2005): 851-874.

Zhou. Tong. "Deterrence Meets a Great Wall." *The Diplomat,* 9 November 2011. http://thediplomat.com/new-leaders-forum/2011/11/09/deterrence-meets-great-wall/ (accessed 6 December 2012).